The
SEVEN PURPOSES

An Experience in
Psychic Phenomena

BY

MARGARET CAMERON

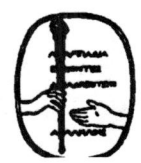

"*That is what we hope to establish as a recognized truth in your life there; that a force as yet unknown to science is operating between the planes, and can be developed and used in your life.*"

"*A force compared to which electricity is spring water.*"

"*Some day your scientists will discover and prove by experiment certain laws now unrecognized.*"

"*If you will only believe and know that I am not dead.*"

"*Come, all ye who struggle and strive! Perceive once and forever the purpose of life. Join now the forces of construction, and bring to all men brotherhood.*"

"*A great brotherhood is only possible when its component parts are great.*"

"*Forget the class and remember the man. Forget the price and remember the pearl. Forget the labor and remember the fruit. Forget the temple and remember God.*"

INTRODUCTION

TWENTY-FIVE years or more ago my attention was attracted to the entertaining possibilities of a planchette, and, like other young persons, I played with one at intervals for several years. Like others, also, I speculated concerning the source of the remarkable statements sometimes obtained in this way, but the assumption that these statements were dictated by disembodied personalities always seemed to me rather absurd.

At no time has my interest in the matter been sufficient to lead me to read anything describing or discussing psychic phenomena, with the exception of an occasional magazine article. Neither have I read philosophies to any extent. I have been always a busy person, taking life at first hand, without much regard to what students have said about it. Such faith as I have had in anything, human or divine, has been based upon works, and, without convincing demonstration, it has been impossible for me to be sure that individual life continued.

After the beginning of the war, however, when interest in the possible survival of the individual was so suddenly and pathetically increased, and one heard on every hand of attempts to establish communication with those gone before, I resolved to experiment again with planchette; but it was not until our friend V— expressed a desire to try it with me, sometime in 1917, that I really bought one. For almost a year it lay untouched in its box, and when finally we found opportunity to test it we had no success. It did not move from the spot where we placed it, and I made no attempt to try it alone.

Several weeks later, two friends, Mrs. Wylie and Miss Gaylord, told me that they had been making efforts, through some one near their home, to get into touch with their brother Frederick, with results they thought promising. A day or two later we tried planchette together, with some success. It moved briskly, wrote "Frederick . . . mother . . . love . . . happy . . ." and other detached words. It also persisted in making little circles, perhaps two inches in diameter, the pencil tracing the circumference again and again. This was so often repeated that Mrs. Wylie thought it might be a symbol, but could obtain no satisfactory reply to questions about it.

My friends went home without renewing the experiment, and my interest was not greatly stimulated. It seemed quite probable that the words written had reflected the thoughts and desires of Frederick's sisters, and that the whole episode could be explained by the theory of unconscious response by the muscles of the hand to the prompting of the subconscious mind. I had dismissed the matter, as far as my own participation in it was concerned, when a letter came from Mrs. Gaylord, saying that her daughters had told her I had "mediumistic power," and suggesting that I might be able to help her.

I knew that the exceeding bitterness of her grief lay, not in the separation from her only son, but in her inability to believe that his identity and development continued, and that the assurance that he had not "gone out, like a snuffed candle," as she afterward expressed it, would bring her the greatest—indeed, the only possible comfort. Therefore I replied at once that while I had no reason to believe that I possessed "mediumistic power" to the slightest degree, I would make further experiments, at the same time warning her that the attempt would probably prove fruitless.

The following pages contain a partial history of the result. It was soon evident that certain of these revelations were of too great moment to be withheld from public knowledge. In addition, while much of the more intimate personal matter has been omitted, most of those to whom these messages were given have felt impelled to share, in this tragic time, the comfort and assurance of their conviction, and have voluntarily yielded their privacy, hoping thereby to bring to those in sorrow an added faith in the continuance of personality, with all that this implies.

To facilitate reference, and to avoid breaking the sequence of the twelve impersonal communications forming the basis of the whole revelation, this report has been arranged in three parts. First, the genesis and rapid development of the individual message, brief at first, and purely personal, but growing both in volume and in import with each day. Second, the Lessons. Third, additional individual messages, no less personal in their original application than the first, but more impressive in their wider human appeal and significance, illuminating and emphasizing the meaning of the Lessons.

For obvious reasons, the names and initials used have been substituted for those of the persons involved, with three or four exceptions.

Part I

"That is the eternal battle, between the purposes of progress and building, and the purposes of disintegration. It goes on in your life, and it goes on less bitterly in ours. Help me build as we began, toward the great unity."

"This is the battle to which we call you and all who are for progress."

THE SEVEN PURPOSES

I

MY first serious attempt to establish communication through planchette with a person or persons in a life beyond ours was made Sunday morning, March 3, 1918. Not so very serious an attempt, either, for I anticipated no success, and was not without a humorous appreciation of my position, sitting with my hand on a toy, inviting communication with celestial powers. I remember laughing a little, as I pictured the sardonic glee with which certain of my friends would be likely to regard such a proceeding.

Perhaps this is as good a time as any to say that I was seeking a stranger. I never saw Frederick. When our friendship with his parents began they lived in one city, we in another, and he in a third and more distant one, where he was first a reporter and later a political and editorial writer on the staff of a leading newspaper. I knew that he was young, successful,

3

a bachelor, and singularly devoted to his family, as they to him. But his habits of thought and speech had never been described to me, at first because it was expected that we would meet, and in the much closer intimacy of our later acquaintance, because the pain of his loss was so poignant that no member of the family could speak of him with composure. I had never seen a photograph of him, even.

After perhaps twenty minutes, during which planchette did not move, I left the paper—a roll of blank wall-paper, called lining-paper, which I found years ago to offer the most continuous and satisfactory surface for use with planchette—spread over the table, and went into another room, intending to return later. But I forgot it, and only when I was putting things in order for the night did I re-enter that room and remember my promise to Mrs. Gaylord. I decided to make one more attempt, that I might be able to tell her positively that I had been unsuccessful. All other members of the household were away—Cass at Atlantic City, recuperating from an illness—and I was entirely alone in the apartment.

For some minutes planchette was motionless, but almost immediately I felt the curious sense of vitality, very difficult to describe, that precedes movement. It is like touching something alive and feeling its latent power. Presently it began to move. Unfortunately no exact record of those first messages was kept, and this report of them is taken from my letters to Cass, written immediately after each interview, and from the typewritten record begun a week or ten days afterward, in which was included what I could remember of details not written to him. At first there was little capitalization, but within a few days capitals were used freely. The punctuation throughout has been added, except in cases noted.

From a letter dated Monday morning, March 4th:

. . . Instead of doing the usual loop sort of thing, it made straight runs across the table. I asked, "Are you ready to write?" "Yes." Then, as nearly as I can remember, it went like this:

"Are you Frederick?" "No."

"Are you Mary Kendal?" "No."

"Are you Anne Lowe?" [1] "No."

"Did I know you in life here?" "Yes."

"Recently?" "No."

"Are you my father?" At this it ran sharply toward me, point first, but for some time did not reply, perhaps because I so hoped it would write "yes." Eventually, however,

[1] These names occurred to me, because these three persons left us within a twelvemonth, about three years ago, and all were either friends or closely identified with friends of ours.

it wrote a very clear and uncompromising "No."

"Can you tell me who you are?" "Yes. Mary."

"Mary Kendal?" "No."

"Which Mary? What Mary?" "Mary . . ." followed by a character that might have been either K or H, but looked more like K.

"Mary Kendal?" "No."

"Tell me again." "Mary K."

"Mary K.?" "Yes." Planchette was down at the lower right-hand corner of the table when I asked the last question, and it swung to the center, writing that "yes" very quickly and firmly.

"*My* Mary K.?" "Yes . . . yes . . . yes."

Her name was Mary Katherine M——, but I always called her Mary K. She has been dead sixteen years or more. Over and over she insisted that she was Mary K. Sometimes, in pauses, with the casters hardly moving at all, the thing would write "Mary," in tiny script, but round and clear.

I asked if there were any message, and it wrote, "Mon. . . ," trailing off into a series of waves, a good many times. I guessed Monday . . . money . . . Mons. . . , but always the answer was, "No." Finally it wrote "man" very clearly. I could not get more for quite a while. Finally came, "Many thanks."

"Thanks for what?" "For knowing."

I asked if Frederick or Anne were there. "No."

"Any message?" "Yes."

"For whom?" "Broth . . .," trailing off again. This several times. "Brother?" "Yes."

"Where?" "Albany."

"His name?" "James."

"James M——?" "No." This was confusing.

"Where?" Beginning apparently with U, the writing trailed off. Finally made out "United . . .," but no more. Then I remembered that Mary K.'s only brother was killed in an accident, years before she went over herself. I said so, and the thing began making loops. That used to be planchette's way of laughing at me.

"Why did you say that?" "Joke." This was not at all like Mary K. She had a fine mind and was not given to buffoonery. I have since thought that she might have been trying to get over a message to some other person's brother.[1]

". . . Can you get word from Frederick Gaylord?" "Yes."[2]

[1] I now believe that this was Annie Manning's first interruption.
[2] I had asked whether she knew any of the three persons previously mentioned, and each time she had replied in the negative.

7

"Will you come again?" "Yes."

"Have you been trying all these years to get into touch with me?" "No."

"Will you help me make a bridge between those on your side and those here?" "No." Then immediately it went back and wrote, "Yes," over the "No." Very curious.

After a long pause, I said I would go to bed, if there were nothing more, and it wrote, quickly, "Go." I said, "Good night." "Good night. God bless you." I asked again if this were Mary K., and got the same quick "Yes." Then I put planchette away and came out to my room. It was one o'clock. Three before I went to sleep. Can you imagine anything more weird than my sitting here alone in the middle of the night, with that thing fairly racing under my fingers part of the time, insisting it was nobody I expected? Claiming to be a very dear old friend, but the last I should expect under the circumstances. It was certainly queer, but I am very sure something outside of myself was doing it. I shall try again to-night.

From a letter dated Monday evening, March 4th:

I have just had another amazing try at planchette. This time it was Mary Kendal, writing one word at a time. "Let . . . Manse [1]

[1] Her husband, Mansfield Kendal.

... know ... I ... am ... here. ...." She gave
me several intimate messages for him, and when
I finally said I would write and ask him to
come, so she could tell him herself, she wrote,
"Yes ... yes ... yes," very quickly.

What do you make of this? Isn't it the
queerest thing you ever heard of? In the
midst of her talk, another hand took hold, very
brisk and energetic.

"Not Mary?" "No."

"Perhaps Frederick?" "Yes."

"Message?" "Yes. Mother."

"Anything more?" "Happy."

"More yet?" "Only love."

Then he was gone, and Mary came again,
writing "Miss A——, messenger," many times.
Later, Frederick interrupted to write one word,
"family."[1] Then another hand began writing "Annie Manning," over and over, and,
"tell Manning." I said that I knew no
Manning. How find him? Answer, "Question." I did not know what that meant. ....
There was a lot more, but I am too tired to
write it to-night.

B—— Gaylord telephoned to-night. She is
either coming to New York Thursday or going
to Atlantic City, if I am there. .... This is the

---

[1] I have since learned that this was characteristic of him. His
letters home frequently began: "Dear Family."

most amazing thing that ever happened to me!
To-night it was as if several were trying to
talk at once. I am almost afraid to have
B. G. come, yet it was for her sake that I began this. It seems too indefinite and unsatisfactory. But at least she can be sure I am not
faking it. Something outside of me does it.

That same evening I wrote to Mansfield
Kendal, though what his attitude toward this
situation would be I could not even guess.
We had known him well for several years, but
our numerous discussions had never touched
questions of religious faith and a future life. A
man of extensive reading and of wide interests,
supplemented by long residence abroad, he has
been engaged for years in the executive conduct
of large engineering and agricultural enterprises.
I knew him to be intellectually open-minded.
But I also knew him to be a devoted adherent
of the orthodox Church, giving much time and
thought to its support, and I was afraid that
an assumption on my part of ability to communicate with the departed might offend some
deep and reverent sense in him. Therefore,
while I wrote him fully of my surprising experience, giving him Mary's messages, I promised at the same time never to force the subject in conversation, should he prefer not to

discuss it. Subsequently, impelled by Mary's continued insistence, I wrote several other letters to him, which, like the first, were sent to his club in New York City, as I knew him to be traveling in the Middle West and thought they would reach him more quickly in this way than if sent to his business headquarters in the South.

Thus, curiously, I found myself vicariously engaged in a double search for a mother on this plane seeking her son on the next, and for a wife on the next plane seeking her husband here, and it is significant that, of the two, Mary Kendal was the more insistent. As she said, later, "We know how much it means."

From a letter to Cass, dated Tuesday morning, March 5th:

Another evening with Mary! H. dined with me. I told her something about planchette, and she wanted to see it work. . . . This time it wrote, "Mary Kendal," at once, and, "Tell Manse I love him. . . . Tell him Miss A—— is messenger from some one he knows. . . . Mentally beautiful people are fearless. . . . Faith is fearlessness. . . . Mannerisms are essential to recognition." Some of these took a long time to work out.

H. asked, "Do you mind my being here?" "Excellent portent."

I asked why. "Intellectual interest."

11

H. said, "You mean that you are glad to have intelligent people interested?" "Yes."

When we were talking about H.'s interest, it wrote, "Tell others." This was repeated several times. "I am a missionary," came as clearly as I have written it here. We asked if she meant a missionary from that life to this. "Yes." At the end she again urged H. to tell others. I laughed, saying, "Tell as many others as you like about the experience, but don't tell too many that it came through me." "Sorry."

"Sorry that I am unwilling to be overwhelmed by a flood of curiosity and hysteria?" "Sorrow." I said I would be glad to help people in sorrow. "Sorrowful people suffer." Isn't that like Mary Kendal?

When H. was leaving, it wrote: "Good night. Tell others."

After she had gone I went back, and got another movement entirely. "Frederick?" "Yes." He seems to have more difficulty in writing than she does. Is very clear at first, but becomes illegible sooner.

"Do you know that your mother is coming?" "Yes. . . . Wish to make her at peace." I said I wished to make her at peace, too, and would do all I could, and he wrote, "Thank you."

As has been said, Cass had been ill, and his

improvement after going to Atlantic City had not been as rapid as we had hoped it might be. A letter received from him on Tuesday reported a slight relapse, and promised a telegram on Wednesday. It had been arranged that I should join him if he needed me.

From a letter dated Wednesday evening, March 6th:

Your letter and wire both came after four, though the letters usually arrive with the first mail in the morning. I was getting a little anxious. Went to planchette and asked Mary Kendal whether she knew anything about you. She said you were better to-day and that a letter was coming, but that I must go to Atlantic City.[1]

Frederick also came, seeming very anxious lest the meeting with his mother fail. Wrote "message" several times, and by dint of some questioning I found it was not a message he wished to send, but one he wished me to send to her about coming at once. Wrote of her "mental anguish," an expression I never should have used myself, and wanted her to join me at Atlantic City. Knew nothing about you, but was keen to meet her.

Later, he seemed to go, and Mary Kendal

[1] Several hours later I read Cass's letter and telegram to his physician, who advised me to go at once to Atlantic City.

wrote a little. Then came something very hard to get. Over and over we tried. "Com ...come...comf...comp...." I suggested various words. Always the answer was "No." Finally, very clearly and slowly, "Comfort dear Mother." After the M of the last word I expected Manse, as I thought Mary was still writing. When it proved to be "Mother," I said, "Is this Frederick?" "Yes." I promised again to do all I could. He wrote, "Thank you," and went.

It is an amazing experience! ... To sit all alone here and have that foolish toy move firmly and definitely under my hands, write things I have to puzzle out, sign names of persons who are what we call "dead," and beg me to send messages to those they love— all this is startling and deeply impressive. Deeply moving.

The next day I joined Cass at Atlantic City. He had never seen a planchette used, and was much interested in the whole matter. In the evening we experimented, and "Mary Kendal" was written at once.

He exclaimed, "God bless you, Mary Kendal!"

"God bless you, too. Tell Manse I love him. Don't fail to tell him that." During all the preceding days this had been her constant plea. Repeatedly I assured her that I had told him, and as often she urged, "Tell him again."

Then came a strong, brisk movement, to and fro, for a space of about five inches. I asked if this were Frederick, and received an affirmative answer, after which planchette ran about, as if in uncontrollable excitement, presently pausing to write:

"You are a trump!" We laughed, and he added, "You bet!"

As we had never known Frederick, and were unaware at that time of the continuance of what some one familiar with this experience has defined as "the subtleties of personality," this enthusiastic use of slang was startling.

When I asked if he had thought I would fail him, he replied, "No, but I was afraid Mother would not come."

[The next day Mrs. Gaylord told me that when Frederick begged me, on Wednesday, to send her a message about coming at once, she had almost decided to postpone her visit until after our return to New York.]

More running about followed, during which Cass said that it was a pity to obliterate the earlier messages in that way. Planchette then swung back to a clear space and wrote clearly, "Mother is coming!" Beneath this, the bow·

knot flourish we have since learned to associate with Frederick.

"You are a brick!" was a later comment. When Cass said he had thought the last word would be friend, Frederick concluded: "Friend, too. Thank you a million times."

An interesting, but rather confusing, feature of these earlier communications was the constant interruption by Annie Manning. On all occasions, frequently even breaking into messages from some other person, she wrote her name and her one request, "Tell Manning." During this period, also, I repeatedly asked Frederick to give me a message for his father, and was unable to account for his invariable refusal.

Once, I asked Mary Kendal if she had no message for me, personally, and she returned, "Yes, believe," which seemed, at the moment, somewhat cryptic, though the relation of my faith to the full development of this intercourse was afterward explained.

Thursday night, at the end of the fifth day, I was fairly certain that I had established communication with three definite and recognizable personalities on the next plane, but I dreaded Mrs. Gaylord's arrival the following day, lest these fragmentary messages fail either to convince or to comfort her.

II

THE next morning, Friday, March 8th, before giving Frederick an opportunity to communicate with his mother, I read her my letters to Cass, wishing her to know just what had occurred and my attitude toward it. Then we turned to planchette.

From this point, the account is taken from the original manuscript. At first we did not realize the importance of writing in our questions, some of which we were unable to remember later. During those first days, also, the messages were sometimes confused by other messages written over them, or by lines and circles done in apparent excitement and joy, and were impossible to decipher afterward.

Frederick's writing, from the first moment with his mother, was quick and firm—at that time the most rapid and consecutive I had ever seen done through planchette, although in comparison with later communications these were slow and fragmentary.

"Mother dearest," he began, immediately,

without question or comment from either of us.

She told me that this had been his name for her, which I had not known. He went on, writing eagerly, with brief pauses between phrases.

"I am here, dearest. . . . Just believe. . . . Mother, you do believe, don't you? . . . Tell me you do."

After replying to some questions, he began making the small circles first noticed during the preliminary episode when his sisters were in New York. I asked what they meant.

"Joy. . . . Don't fail to make her believe." I reminded him that this was his responsibility, and he added, "You and I."

A question of which there is no record drew this reply: "Yes, busy every minute. . . . Work is so interesting. . . . I love you just the same. . . . Go home when I can. . . . Tell Dad I am with him . . . helping all I can . . . I am so glad you came. . . . I was afraid you would not. . . . Go home in peace, Mother dearest. I am alive and happy and busy and well."

She said it was like him to sum it all up that way.

"Of course it is like me. It is 'me.'"

Some personal comment concerning members

of the family followed, in the midst of which Annie Manning interrupted with her invariable, "Tell Manning." Asked if she had any connection with the Gaylord family, she said, "No, good-by," and Frederick resumed his sentence where it had been broken off.

Throughout this and subsequent interviews Mrs. Gaylord and I kept up a running conversation, impossible to reproduce here—my hand still resting on planchette—to which Frederick frequently contributed a remark, precisely as if he had been present in the flesh. Again, he would break a pause by addressing some characteristic statement or appeal to his mother, sometimes, she told me afterward, answering her unspoken thought.

Over and over he begged her to say that she was convinced of his presence and identity, and at last she gave him this assurance.

"Oh, thank God!" He made strong circles, before running up to a clear space some inches above, to add, "Tell Dad."

For the first time, a possible explanation of his inexorable refusal to give me a message for his father occurred to me, and when I asked, he said, "Yes, I want to reach them through her."

He told her not to think of him as he had been during the months of his last illness, saying: "Forget all that. It is over, and I am well and strong, and happier than ever—now." When we wondered whether it had distressed him to be unable to communicate with his family, he said, "Yes, I needed that."

"Will you talk every day, you and she?" he asked, presently. "Thank you."

"Mrs. Gaylord, Frederick is a fine force," followed immediately, in a more running script, and when I said this must be Mary Kendal, the answer was: "Yes. Tell Manse I love him. . . . Tell him again."

"He doesn't need to be told that," I assured her, as I had so many times before.

And again she returned: "Yes, he does. There are reasons. Tell him." I promised to write to him once more, and she continued: "Mrs. Gaylord, Frederick wants you to be sure that he is doing more here than he could there. You should not grieve for that, should you? You have a fearless mind in other things. Trust for that. Good-by."

"Mother dearest, that was Mrs. Kendal," Frederick resumed, with his more vigorous movement. "She is a missionary, and a fine force."

Noticing the repetition of this word, I asked, "You say force, not spirit?"

"No, force is what moves things."

To his mother's inquiry about a friend, he replied: "He is here with me, working. Bob's little girl is here, too." She told me that a medium visited by his sisters had described him with a little girl, saying that he wanted them to "tell Bob." [I had heard this from them, also, and the subject recurred later.]

"Yes," he acquiesced. "Same child."

When she expressed her belief that he was still alive and growing, promising that she would be happier in future, he said: "Thank you, Mother dearest. That is all I need. Tell Dad to be happy, too. I am with him. He has not lost a son. I am better and bigger and more useful than I ever could have been there, but I have been sorry you suffered so much."

"Have you been trying recently to let us know you were with us?" she inquired.

"Yes, for months. At first I could not."

He said that Mary Kendal had found him for us, and when I mentioned that Mary K. had come first to me, he explained: "Yes, she is more used to it. She found Mrs. Kendal, and she told me."

"You had better get your lunch," he suggested, after a pause, rousing us from our complete absorption to a consciousness that it was late. Mrs. Gaylord denied being hungry,

3

but he warned her — characteristically, I learned afterward, "You will have a headache, Mother dearest, if you don't."

After luncheon we went out for a walk, and then to our respective rooms to rest, the morning having been fatiguing in its emotional strain. Planchette and paper had been left in Mrs. Gaylord's room, and in the afternoon, while Cass and I were still alone, I picked up a lead-pencil and placed its point on a sheet of letter-paper, expecting no response. To my great surprise, I was conscious almost instantly of its vitality. The sensation is comparable to that of holding a quiet, live bird, wrapped in a handkerchief, its energy muffled but palpable. Sometimes this sensation of a current from without is communicated to the hand and arm, sometimes only to the fingers.

In a short time the pencil moved, writing, "Mary Kendal," followed by the usual messages for Manse.

Cass asked whether it annoyed them to be questioned, or interfered with things they might wish to tell us.

"No, it does not interfere. We are here to tell you what we can, but we cannot tell everything. . . . You have the right to know what we can tell you. . . . You are getting nearer the big things every day." This made Cass wonder whether "the big things" would come to us in this life or the next, and she added: "Both. You begin there and keep on growing. As soon as you are ready, big truths are shown to you."

Addressing me, he made some allusion to what "she" had said, suggesting that it seemed to support a theory he had once held, that this world is one of elimination.

"No, it is one of growth," was her answer. "And 'she' is trying to tell you that growth begins there and does not stop. It goes on and on, as long as you are worthy."

"Then unworthiness kills?"

"It does not kill. It defers."

Weeks afterward, it was interesting to turn back to these early pages of the record and find how much of the wide significance of later revelations had been foreshadowed from the first.

"Are you as eager for this communication as we are?"

"We are more eager, because we know how much it means. We know that more truth can be taught this way than any other."

Cass turned to Mrs. Gaylord, who had rejoined us, saying that this seemed to imply that they were our superiors.

"No, we are your elders," said Mary Kendal.

As has generally been the case during these interviews, we were talking among ourselves, frequently going on with our conversation while the pencil wrote. Some one wondered how or why they had time or desire to leave their presumably more important work to talk to us.

"Because we are all humans, after all," Mary responded, "and it is our work to help, just as it is yours. Many people do not want to help, here or there. . . . This life is just a continuation of yours under happier conditions."

"Are you happier there than you were here, Mary?"

"Yes, except for Manse."

Mrs. Gaylord asked whether a man who had loved books, and had always kept himself surrounded by them in this life, would find that interest there.

"No," Mary said, "but we have its equivalent interest."

Mrs. Gaylord then explained that the medium already mentioned had described Frederick to his sisters as surrounded by books.

"He told her that to identify himself, as characteristic."

[In this connection, an incident occurring three months later is interesting.

[One night, about the middle of June, a group of us had been talking for some time, through my pencil, with friends on the next plane, when one of the women announced that she could see distinctly a large man's hand resting upon the hand of a man present.

[The person in question—a hard-headed, practical business man, successfully conducting large affairs—looked startled, saying that he had noticed a peculiar sensation in that hand, and asked whether a friend, whom he named, was actually present.

["Yes," was the reply through the pencil. "R—— saw. I manifested physical attributes for a minute. I have no hands, but I can imagine them and project them in your minds, occasionally."

[No one else saw the hand, and at no other time in my experience has anything of this kind occurred.]

I asked Mary Kendal whether they preferred planchette or pencil, and she said, "It is easier for us this way." Therefore, except on one memorable occasion, all later writing has been done with a pencil.

For the information of persons interested in physical details, it may be explained that I generally use a long pencil, which is held erect, almost at right angles to the paper, the fingers clasping it lightly two or three inches from its point, the hand and arm entirely unsupported.

In the very rapid writing that has sometimes been done, and occasionally in moments of great eagerness or emotion, the force propelling the pencil—which seems to be applied sometimes above, sometimes below my hand—has forced it to a sharply acute angle in relation to the surface of the paper. From the first, I have used right and left hands alternately, and the writing, with exceptions so few as to be negligible, has been done in rather large script on wall-paper, many rolls of which have been covered.

One of the exceptions to the use of wall-paper was this first experiment with a pencil, when loose sheets of letter-paper were used, and as many of them were missing when I tried to assemble them the next day, much of this interview has been lost.

"Frederick, shall we ever have our holidays again?" Mrs. Gaylord asked, in the evening.

"Just as many holidays as you will take," he replied. "I am always there on high days and holidays. Why leave me out?" This was the first time he made an interrogation point. It was traced slowly and with great precision, as if to emphasize his inquiry.

His mother then explained to us that the celebration of certain festivals, which had always been days of family reunion, notably

Christmas and Easter, had been impossible to them since his death. Shortly afterward he expanded this theme.

That night Mrs. Gaylord telegraphed to her husband that she had received messages for him and for the family. She said, as other members of the family have said since, that there was in everything Frederick had written a familiar and convincing sense of his personality, a quality which we were unable to recognize, never having known him.

The next day he announced, buoyantly: "Mother dearest, I am here. Thank you for wiring Dad. Made him happier."

Greatly comforted by the conviction of her son's continued life and development and devotion, Mrs. Gaylord's thought was already turning to other bereaved and suffering mothers, and more than once she expressed her desire to share with them her new knowledge, urging me to make preparations for the publication of the messages she was sure Frederick would give us, to which, for personal reasons, I demurred. We asked Frederick whether he thought it should be published, and he replied in the affirmative. After some discussion, leaving me still unconvinced, he resumed his appeal to his mother.

"You will be happy now, won't you? You

can't be sorry I am so much better off and more useful. I get your thoughts and you get mine, only you don't recognize them always as mine. You will now."

"Is there any way I can know when you are with me?" she asked.

"You will learn, now you know I am there. I can't tell you how, but you will learn. That is part of this big knowledge, dearest. You are both just beginning, but, like other knowledge, growth is rapid, once begun. You will meet skeptics, who will laugh, but don't be disturbed. This is the next big revelation, and you are with the first over the top."

"Are you still interested in the war?" she asked, and the reply came with great vigor.

"Yes. How can anybody help that? It is great and hideous and wonderful, and the salvation of the civilized world. Something had to wake the souls of most men. They have been quiet too long. Growth is always struggle. It is hard struggle there, because you don't see far ahead. We see farther— much farther—and it is easier to climb."

"Was the war the fault of the Germans, or the result of world conditions?"

"Both. The Germans had long been obsessed by a lust of power, and the rest of the world by a lust of ease and money, and individual interests. There has been real unity of purpose only in Germany." When she said that this thought of Germany's unity had been much in her mind of late, he added, quickly, "That was I, Mother dearest, trying to tell you what I could of what I know."

A long talk on personal topics followed, during which he referred to me as a "messenger," explaining Mary Kendal's previous use of the word. By this time, many of the messages were conveyed to my consciousness before the pencil wrote them. Sometimes I had no previous impression of them; sometimes only the meaning reached me, being expressed by the pencil in other phrases; sometimes I knew what the words would be. I mentioned this, with some misgiving, and Frederick dryly remarked: "You are very sensitive for so obstinate a person."

Referring to his earlier statement about Germany, Cass asked: "What would national unity of purpose lead to? Hasn't it elements of great danger?"

"Many men feel that unity of purpose is dangerous, but it is up to men . . . to guide the purpose to sane and right ends. It must come through the awakening of the souls of the people everywhere. We work for that here, because the growth of the part is the growth of the whole. You can help us and all life by working for that unity with us."

This was the first intimation, apparently personal and casual, of that gospel of unity and co-operation so fully developed later.

"Mother dearest, you are normally a builder," he went on, after a little. "Now clear away the débris of things outlived, and begin the new structure with me."

She replied that she had been feeling for some time that she must free her life of many small, insistent demands, and have time to think.

"Not only that, dearest. You must get out of shadow into light. Out of mourning into building. Out of black into color and life. Out of grieving into joy with me in our work together. It is not that I object to black," he continued, when she expressed her unwillingness to lay aside her black dress, "but to a symbol of mourning. Sorrow is not constructive, after it has done its first big work. Leave it behind and go on. Can't you do that? Won't you please try? . . . As for me, this is a great time to be here. Think what this war means here. We are busier than you are. There, I should be in the army, I suppose. I am doing bigger work than that here. Just now, I am on a sort of furlough, to visit with you. That is permitted. But when I go back to work I can't be with you all the time, this way."

"Can you get into touch with my father, who died years ago?" Cass asked. "And do the young stay young, and the old, old?"

"I will try to find your father. Some of us go on into remoter places to work, but almost all of us come back, at intervals. We are tremendously interested in life there, for it is the root and beginning of all our work. When things improve there, they are just that much better here. . . . Age is a matter of experience here, not of time."

"Does your work affect us in this world, or only those joining you?"

"We try constantly to help you with our greater knowledge, but some of you are easier to help than others." This led to a question as to whether all our knowledge here is given to us from his plane, and he went on: "Not all. We help develop what you are willing to work for, if you are really sincere in wanting it. Sincerity is the crowning virtue."

We talked this over, and in the midst of our discussion he interrupted with a question of his own:

"Mother dearest, are you getting tired?" She denied it, but he said, "She is tired," and we talked no more that afternoon.

III

SHORTLY before dinner that night I picked up a pencil again, and "Mary Kendal" was immediately written. It had become customary for her to write her name both at the beginning and at the end of her communication, probably to avoid confusion with Frederick.

"Manse is in New York," she told us, repeating it several times. For some reason I questioned this, and she said: "You must not doubt. He is coming to-night."

"Are you happy, Mary?" Cass asked.

"Very, especially now, since I am with you. You can reach Manzie."

Keenly sympathizing with her eagerness to reach her husband, from whom no word had come, he suggested telephoning to Mansfield at his club, but I demurred, feeling that, if he were there, he would receive my letters and communicate with us, unless, as I began to fear, he preferred not to approach the subject in any way. Repeatedly, however, Mary insisted, "Call him up," and Cass put in the long-distance call accordingly.

"He is there. . . . He will answer," she reiterated again and again, while we waited.

It is impossible to make a fully accurate report of this interview. The messages were confused and broken, and there were many monosyllabic replies to questions not recorded.

At one time we asked about Anne Lowe, and Mary said: "Anne is not here. She is a lovely character. She works for children. . . . Manse is not there. . . . Manse is out. . . . He will answer. . . . He is not there."

Eventually the long-distance operator reported that Mr. Kendal was not at his club and was not expected.

I asked Mary why she had said that he was there, telling her that this was making me doubt my powers of correct transmission, to which she replied that this was better than too much credulity, adding: "Manse is there. . . . He is out of the club. . . . He must be there."

We called up the —— Club a second time and I talked to the clerk, who said Mansfield Kendal was not registered there, nor had they been notified that he was coming. Long afterward we learned that he had expected to be there at that time, but had been detained in the Northwest by business.

Meanwhile, there was much confused writing from Mary. "Manse is in the club. . . . He is not there. . . . He must be there. . . . He is out." Effort to write the name of a city was followed by, "Minneapolis recently. . . . Manse will be there soon."

It was Mansfield Kendal himself who ultimately arrived at a possible explanation of some of these apparent inaccuracies, Mary having explained others meanwhile. But at the time it was all very contradictory and confusing, and after dinner Cass demanded an explanation.

Mary Kendal came at once, admitting that she had been wrong in saying that Mansfield was at the club, and asserting that she "thought he would be."

"Didn't you know?"

"No."

Again the messages are confused and fragmentary. "You must not doubt. . . . He will be there soon . . ." are among those now decipherable, each many times repeated. She seemed profoundly distressed.

To ease the tension, Cass made a little joke, eliciting no response from her, whereupon he asked whether they retained a sense of humor over there.

"Yes, but this is no time for humor. . . . I am so afraid of missing Manse."

Again she urged me to write to him, but I refused, reminding her that I had made every possible advance until some reply to my letters should be received.

"Yes, I know, but it means so much! You will help, won't you?"

Knowing nothing then of the tremendous forces of attraction and repulsion unconsciously put into operation by persons ignorant of their existence, and assuming—not unnaturally—that she must be able to learn at least as much about Mansfield's whereabouts and condition as both she and Frederick evidently knew about ours, I was unable to understand, even dimly, the contradictions of the present situation, and the cloud of it hung over me all that evening and the next day. I was oppressed by a sense of my responsibility in conveying messages from sources seeming suddenly so uncertain.

Following Mary, Frederick came again, his buoyancy undiminished.

"Mother dearest," he began, without question, "Mrs. Kendal is true. She is a fine force." I rather held back on this, and the writing was angular and unyielding. "There are things we cannot explain."

"You have too little faith. Mary Kendal."

This statement was made without preliminary comment, and until she signed her name I thought Frederick was writing. I reminded her that she had made it impossible for me to trust her wholly.

"I am sorry I shook your faith," she said. "I welcome you to this relation, and want you to believe."

"Mother dearest, you know I am here, don't you?" Again Frederick made his own interrogation point. "Because I am, and you will feel my presence more and more clearly as time goes on."

"Do you know all that we want to know?" Cass inquired.

"Not all you want to know. We know more than you do, and will tell you all we can, as soon as you are ready for it." We were uncertain whether this meant mentally and spiritually ready, or that we must learn the conditions through which they can best reach us, and he explained. "We can tell you anything you are prepared to understand, and the more you learn there the better you will do your work here."

"Are you still interested in politics here?" he was asked, a little later.

"Oh yes. But they are in a state of transition that is fearfully difficult to understand or to influence now. The seed has been sown, but the harvest is not yet garnered. Nobody knows what will come of it in this country."

"Are you conscious there of what people here call God?" his mother asked.

"We are conscious of a great purpose. Some of us call it God. I see it as light in dark places. Others see it as power. Others as love. But we all recognize it as a purpose."

At luncheon that day we had spoken of Prof. William James and Sir Frederick Myers, and later in the evening Mrs. Gaylord asked Frederick whether he knew Professor James.

"I know him, but I am not sure he knows me. He is a great force, and many of us go to him for help and instruction. Only one other man has the same sort of power. That is Sir Frederick."

"Are you with people from this world only?" some one asked. "And does everybody go there, or only a certain element?"

"There are people from this world only, but it is as with you, not all people are equally prepared. Growth is easier here if one has earned it there. But not all have earned it, and the penalty for laziness is long struggle. . . . Purgatory is not a bad definition of it. The right to do big work must be earned.

4

Some people have a terrible struggle of it. [Their?] Moral muscles are flabby."

"Do you agree with Mary Kendal that there is humor there, but that this is no time for it?"

"Oh, she didn't mean that! She meant that this particular crisis is not humorous to her. She is deeply concerned to get into touch with him. . . . Good night, Mother dearest. I'll be with you all night."

"Good night," said Mary Kendal. "I'm sorry I upset you."

IV

THE more I thought about the Kendal affair the more perplexing it seemed, and since I could neither question that Mary Kendal and Frederick had actually communicated through me nor believe that she would wilfully deceive me, there seemed no possible explanation of the episode Saturday night, except some unconscious influence of my own mind. By the next afternoon I had almost persuaded myself that the repeated erroneous statements about Mr. Kendal had been induced, in some way not traceable, by my increasing anxiety concerning his reception of the letters I had sent to his club.

After luncheon, we took up the communication again, and immediately, without interrogation, the pencil wrote, "You are a good messenger."

"Who is writing?" I asked.

"Frederick."

"How much of this do I do, and how much is yours?"

"You do very little. Mostly, you lend a hand." This is so literally what I do that we laughed. "You are by nature skeptical," he continued. "Mother dearest, you must not let her make you doubt that I have said all these things."

"It unsettles me when I know what the message is to be before it is written," I persisted. "Do you suggest it to me, or I to you?"

"Sometimes you suggest things to me and I say them," he returned. "Sometimes I don't." This reassured me somewhat, for I had frequently noticed that a thought strongly in my mind seemed to delay the pencil, yet was not written.

Returning for a moment to the discussion of politics, Cass asked: "By reason of our different environment, am I not more interested in large details, and you in large movements?"

"There can be no real movement without a mass of detail. Here we are interested equally in both. They are inseparable."

"You said yesterday that the seed had been sown and the harvest not yet garnered. Has the seed generally been good seed?"

"There is no telling how much of it will come up. There has been seed, good, bad, and indifferent, sown in all sorts of soil.

The crop is not foreordained. We work and hope."

"Is there anything in this life to any degree a counterpart of what you have there?" his mother inquired. "Or is it something so wholly new that we can't even imagine it?"

"It is so much more expansive, so much more beautiful and free, that we can give you no conception of it."

"Perhaps it's better that we shouldn't know," it was suggested; and Frederick's reply seems to hold a hint of humor.

"It might make you envious."

When I wondered what became of suicides, Cass said, "They probably get the purgatory he mentioned yesterday."

"That's what they get; and it's a long, hard road back to mental . . ." The pencil hesitated. After some efforts to write a word beginning with p or f—we were uncertain which—Mrs. Gaylord suggested, "Poise?"

". . . poise. Yes."

"Is there unconsciousness at first, when you go over?" she asked.

"It depends on circumstances and persons. Sometimes there is a period of unconsciousness. I was conscious from the first moment, and so happy to be here." When Cass interpreted this to mean that he greatly preferred

"Mother dearest, you will get what you are asking from me when we are all more accustomed. Margaret is afraid to let me handle her." I said that the Kendal episode the night before had disturbed me, and that I had been careful all day not to yield to any impulse in the pencil unless it were very definite, to which he returned: "That's all right. You be as careful as you like, as long as you don't deny us."

Cass asked whether he could put us in touch with a friend on his plane, one David Bruce.

"Mary Kendal can. That is part of her work. Mother dearest, you won't backslide?"

Mrs. Gaylord turned astonished eyes on me, asking: "Is 'backslide' a part of your ordinary vocabulary?" When I assured her that it was not, she laughed, saying that it was "a Gaylord word." "I'm not sure that I won't backslide when I get home again, away from these daily messages," she said.

"Then you come to us—Margaret and me. We'll fix you!" He drew a circle around this, as if to emphasize it. When she wondered whether she might not find a messenger nearer home to give her occasional help, he added: "You can get help, but you can't trust everybody."

The pencil was moving slowly, with many

44

false starts and delays. I asked whether he would prefer planchette, and he said he would, so his mother went to her room to get it, while Mary Kendal talked to us about Manse. As soon as planchette was placed on the table, however, Frederick took possession again, moving it briskly back and forth, in a space of about six inches, as if warming it up. Mrs. Gaylord was then sitting opposite me, and Cass to the right, some distance away.

Suddenly planchette swung sharply down to the lower right-hand corner of the table, from my position, and addressing Mrs. Gaylord directly—that is, writing from right to left and upside down from my viewpoint, so that his mother sitting opposite me read it as it came—Frederick wrote rapidly and strongly:

"Mother dearest, this is your boy, come back to stay."

We were astounded. Given a fresh surface, planchette raced all over the sheet, in energetic circles and flourishes. It ran toward me, point first, as if it would leap off the table, paused, wheeled, crossed toward Mrs. Gaylord, retreated, darted to where her hand lay on the papers, followed as she moved it, and then resumed its apparently meaningless tracing of angles and circles. When I said that I did not understand this performance, the reply came with a whirl, followed by one of his big flourishes.

"I am trying to show you that I am running this myself!" Then, very rapidly, upside down again to me: "You can't doubt this. Even Margaret can't doubt this."

"I haven't doubted that you were here, Frederick," I said.

"No, but you've got to believe in me."

Again I placed the instrument at my left, in readiness to write, as usual, across the sheet, but he had not finished. Swinging down to the right, and moving toward the left, once more reversed from my point of view, he wrote: "Mother dearest." Then he ran to the upper right-hand corner and wrote along that edge of the table: "Now I'll do it this way, Mr. L——." In circles and flourishes he crossed, to write along the left edge: "Now I'll do it this way." Up then, to the edge opposite me. "Now I'll do it this way."

By this time the paper was completely covered with interlacing lines and words, except a narrow margin along the right edge. Sliding over to this, he wrote, slowly, "Now are you convinced?"

We were amazed, breathless, and all somewhat moved by his determination to demonstrate his presence.

Circling again to the center, already so covered with lines that we had to watch the pencil-point to make out the message, he said: "Now get the pencil."

"Did I show you then who is running this?" he demanded, when I had complied with his request. "Mother dearest, when you are inclined to backslide, remember that little exhibition, and ask yourself how you can doubt any manifestation of me that you perceive."

Mrs. Gaylord said that it was peculiarly characteristic of Frederick to insist upon making his point, and in one way or another to succeed.

"Dad won't need to see that," Frederick stated, when Cass wished that his father might have witnessed this extraordinary performance, "but if he does, I'll do it for him with trimmings. . . . He has not lost a son in any but the most superficial sense. Tell Sis I'll do stunts for her, too, if she'll come where Margaret is, and Babe can have her own show, too."

Again Mrs. Gaylord gasped, for he had used his own intimate names for his sisters, neither of which I had ever heard before.

"Now we re really getting down to business," he remarked, presently. "I had to convince Margaret before she would loosen up." Cass began to explain that it had not been necessary to convince me, but before he was fairly started the pencil ran on: "Yes, it was. She didn't quite believe I was running this show. Now she's nice and amenable." Verily, all resistance had been taken out of me! Thereafter he had his own way with the pencil.

Cass began another question, but broke off, saying that it was not fair to keep Frederick answering impersonal inquiries when he wanted to talk to his mother.

"That's what it's all for," was the candid admission. "The L——s are all right, but it's for Mother dearest and the Family that I'm here. . . . This isn't exactly what religious people call heaven, but it is life eternal in the biggest sense. But I can't be quite happy in it unless you whom I love so much are happy, too. Don't you backslide! Only let me have a chance, and I'll keep you convinced; but doubt is the hardest thing to combat because it destroys the very proof we are trying to bring against it. Believe every suggestion of me until it is proved false."

One of us asked whether their greatest difficulties in communicating with us were caused by doubt or by dishonest messengers.

"Both. It is hard to find a good messenger,

but, having found one, doubt is apt to destroy all his work."

"All four points of the compass, Mother dearest." This we took to be an allusion to his writing along the four edges of the table, earlier in the evening. "You see, we have not much time left, and you must go home fortified and happy, and glad for yourself and me. . . . It will mean a lot to Dad. He has thought I was in some remote and far-off heaven, and he will like to know that we are working more nearly shoulder to shoulder than ever before, as we are in some ways. . . . I want to talk to him straight." Long afterward one of his sisters told me that "shoulder to shoulder" was a characteristic phrase of Frederick's.

Again sliding over to the lower right-hand corner, he wrote quickly, in big swinging script, upside down to me: "Mother dearest, don't forget the four points of the compass. I want you to remember that I am your boy come back. Not lost at all. Please remember that."

When a fresh surface offered and the pencil was placed at my left, as usual, he said, "No," and swung once more down to the right, writing quickly and firmly toward the left and upside down to me.

THE SEVEN PURPOSES

"I am going to write a little letter to Dad and the girls. I love them just as well as ever, and it hurts me to have them think I am not alive and loving them, because I know they still love me.

"FREDERICK."

Although the movement in this reversed writing is rapid and definite, as if great energy were exerted to accomplish it, it is extremely difficult to follow, perhaps because the muscles of the hand are accustomed to move from left to right in writing, or because the mind instinctively resists a movement it cannot readily understand.

V

THE next day (Monday, March 11th) we all returned to New York together, Mrs. Gaylord rejoining us in the evening, after dining with other friends.

Before her arrival, we talked a little to Mary Kendal, who was still uneasy about the failure to reach her husband, from whom no word had come. We asked if she knew David Bruce, and she replied: "No, but he is here, and most of us know what he does. He is a sweet force."

When Mrs. Gaylord came, we told her of this characterization, after some personal talk with Frederick, and at once he took up the suggestion.

"Mother dearest, you are a sweet force, too. Help me build a structure of strength, which is Dad, sweetness, which is you, and illumination, which is my part."

We remembered then his asking her to "clear away the débris of things outlived and begin the new structure with me," but not until greater revelations followed did we understand fully what he meant.

A little later he said of his father: "He will discover that I am more a force than ever, and then he will be as proud as men who have sons 'over there.' . . . Should you prefer a son in the trenches or in the place of accomplished peace? . . . I am nearer you now than I have ever been before, but the price of that is apparent separation. Your life knows no such companionship as ours can be now, but that is possible only at the cost of apparent and visible contact. This is gain, not loss. You are questioning that, but trust me. I know. You can't even guess what this means to all of us, Sis and Babe and Dad and you and
FREDERICK."

His name was dropped a line, like a signature.

It was coming slowly, with hesitations and false starts, and I asked: "Are you tired, Frederick? Or am I?"

"Both," he said. "This is not the simplest thing I ever did. . . . I am not tired, as you understand weariness, but it is easier sometimes to get things through than others."

The next evening—the last we had with Frederick at that time—his first messages were personal, expressing his desire to "talk straight" to other members of the family.

"But there's no hurry," he went on. "We've all eternity together now. . . . Only one thing can separate us. If you doubt my existence, I shall still exist, but your doubt will destroy the thread that links us like a telegraph-wire, only more closely and warmly. So you must not backslide, for my sake as well as your own."

"Why don't you stay on?" he asked presently. "I can reach you, but not so definitely for a while to your sense, and actual speech with you is keen joy. Tell ~~Dad~~ . . . ."—the erasure is his own—". . . . the family I want to talk to them, too. Let's have a reunion. One that won't leave me out. I want to be in." Rapidly and strongly, he underlined the last words three times.

His mother promised that the family festivals should be held again, in the full consciousness that he was there with them.

"Thank you, Mother dearest. You don't know how we hate being left out." When she explained that they were "left out" ignorantly, rather than intentionally, he continued: "No, we know you don't mean to leave us out. But you—and we, too—would be so much happier if you knew we were there and we could know you were not grieving. You see, we are really nearer to you than you are to each other, and only memory tells us why you grieve. There is no reason for grief in what you call death and we call knowledge."

"Why hasn't all this been told to us before?" she demanded. "It was cruel not to let us know it!"

"As I wrote you the other day, not everybody has been prepared for the knowledge. It is known only to the few—those first over the top I spoke of. But it will be the next great revelation. As well say it was cruel not to have known chloroform in the Middle Ages, when it was sorely needed, or wireless telegraphy in the Napoleonic wars. There is an evolution of soul, as well as of biology and chemistry. Many fine souls have still lacked this peculiar preparation."

This started a little discussion between us. One said that many persons had lost faith in the orthodox religions, thus making the need of a new revelation great. Another spoke disparagingly of the modern theory of a pervasive and impersonal energy, from which we come and to which we return, losing individuality. At this point Frederick took the lead again.

"Don't you let them fool you! There is no such thing as Bergson's stream of energy, unless every individual of us is a well-defined drop in the stream. That is all a philosopher's dream, coated with poetry and tinctured with science."

Mrs. Gaylord said she had never heard of Frederick's reading Bergson, and I mentioned that I had read nothing of his, except one article in a review.

"I never read Bergson, either, but you could not live in the world, or pick up a Sunday supplement, some years ago, without encountering that stream of energy."

"There speaks the newspaper man!" his mother said, laughing.

During all these talks with Frederick he had frequently made the little retraced circle, which we had been told meant joy. He made it again now, with vigor, and some one suggested that he seemed excited.

"Wouldn't it excite you to get into actual touch with your family, after long doubt and pain? I am no angel, you know, and thank God I am not above being excited. When I am I will be dead!" Again he underscored a word.

Mrs. Gaylord spoke of her feeling of his presence, of his characteristic personality, saying that he seemed "just the same."

"Plus, Mother dear. You'd like me better now. I don't mean that I am perfect, you know. I've got more to learn than I ever knew existed, but I can see ahead now. And you would like me better. . . . I didn't say love me better," he added.

We talked about the force moving the pencil, which on this occasion was very strongly applied, though I was greatly fatigued by the efforts of the past few days, and I asked Frederick whether he could move it without my co-operation. But he said, "Only as you hold it." To a suggestion that he expressed himself not through the pencil, but through me, he replied, "She is like the battery."

From the first Mrs. Gaylord had been experimenting with planchette and pencil, hoping to establish direct communication with Frederick. While placing more emphasis on a possible communion of thought, without material aid, he had encouraged these efforts. "Mother, you can do it, I am sure," he said once, "but don't expect much fluency for some time. I have not written except through Margaret yet, but they tell me she is exceptionally sensitive as a messenger."

Referring to this, he was asked whether others, not known to me personally, had desired to communicate through me, and replied: "No, but they have watched her, this last week." Ten days later, when the most amazing of all the communications began to come, we remembered this. After enumerating some of the qualifications of a good messenger, he said: "When that combination is found we are all interested, if we want to reach our own people."

"Are you over there especially interested in reaching your own families and friends, or in reaching persons who might be interested in the possibility of these communications?"

"Both. But if you have ever been unable to communicate with those you love, for months and years, and have known they were suffering, then you know which interest is keenest. The one is immediate and urgent, the other more or less a matter of evolution."

"Shall I try to talk to some of you occasionally?" I asked. "Or shall I wait for a call?"

"You are over the top. We shall be glad to come."

"Can you let me know, if you have something to say through me?"

"Not always. Sometimes we can suggest the thought to you."

Since that time, however, a more perfect connection has been established and I am often conscious of a definite summons. On these occasions the pencil starts at once, generally with great vigor, and almost always writes some message not conveyed to my consciousness except as I spell it out after the pencil.

Toward the end of the evening, when Mrs. Gaylord had suggested going back to her hotel, the pencil made a little circle and some apparently aimless marks inside it.

"Is this Frederick?" I asked, wondering at indecision from him.

"Yes. I want to do something Mother can't forget. . . . You don't need any more fancy stunts, do you?"

She said she did not, but that she was very tired and could stay no longer.

"Oh, don't go!" he begged. "I'll go with you, but I like gassing this way." Another characteristic phrase, she said.

After some further assurances of his frequent presence and constant watchfulness, she said she really must go. Frederick then moved the pencil down to the right corner again, and wrote, very clearly and carefully, one more "upside-down" message—a touching little message of love to "dear Dad and the girls," which he signed, "Your boy, Frederick."

The next day Mrs. Gaylord went home, where she immediately destroyed all her black-bordered cards and stationery and similar symbols of mourning. She wrote me that she felt it was false and wicked to mourn for a son as vitally alive and happy as she now knew Frederick to be.

VI

ONE of my letters to Mr. Kendal had been marked "Urgent." On the day of Mrs. Gaylord's departure a telegram came from him, asking that a duplicate of this letter be sent to him at Chicago. It developed later that all my missives, after some delay, had been forwarded from his club to his business address in the South, where, owing to the uncertainty of his plans, his secretary had held them, notifying him by wire of the one evidently demanding immediate attention.

After some hesitation—reluctant to shock him by a bald and startling announcement unaccompanied by any explanation of a situation concerning which I was convinced he would be skeptical, if not wholly unsympathetic, and yet impelled by his wife's distressed insistence to reach him before he should go South again—I telegraphed him that I had reason to believe I had been in direct communication for several days with Mary and others, and asked him to return *via* New York, if possible.

Early that evening I took up a pencil, which moved at once.

"Manzie has your message."

This could be no one but Mary Kendal. To my inquiry concerning his reception of my telegram she replied: "He is startled. He is wiring you." An expression of her happiness followed, concluding, "He is thinking of me . . . and I can help him."

"Can't you help him unless he is thinking of you?"

Apparently this presented difficulties, but after long effort and many false starts she achieved what I felt to be only a part of the answer she had intended. "On power I can."

"You mean that you can influence his work? His strength, or accomplishment?"

"Yes, but not his heart and soul." After assurances that he would come soon, she thanked me touchingly.

Later in the evening she said, "Manzie is so amazed!" When I asked whether he believed it, she returned: "He does now. He has thought. . . ." Details personal to him followed.

Still later I asked whether Mr. Kendal had telegraphed me, and she said that he had not, though he had intended to do so. As a matter of fact, he had not at that time received my telegram, but he afterward told me that when it reached him, twelve hours later, his reactions were exactly as she had described them. Also, his intention of telegraphing me immediately was delayed several hours by business necessities. This is one of several instances when a difference of plane has seemed to enable them to look ahead for a limited space and foretell events.

The next morning, for the first time in ten days, the pencil was merely a piece of dead wood between my fingers, without impulse. After long delay it moved slowly, making light circles, but no words came.

I knew that Mrs. Gaylord had intended to make an effort that day to get into touch with Frederick through a semi-professional medium in her vicinity, and in the evening I took up a pencil, wondering whether we could learn what success had attended the attempt.

"Mary."

Supposing this to be Mary Kendal, I made some allusion to Mansfield, and was immediately corrected.

"No. Mary K."

This was surprising, as it was the first time she had responded since my initial effort to

establish this intercourse. She said that Mary
Kendal was not present, and that Frederick
had met his mother at Mrs. Z——'s, with results only partially satisfactory—which letters from the Gaylord family afterward verified. We suggested that this might have been
discouraging, and she replied: "Discouragement is not for Frederick."

"How do you know so much about Frederick
now?" I asked. "Ten days ago you said you
did not know him."

"Mrs. Kendal interested me in him. He is
for justice, light, and progress. My work,
too."

To my expressed hope that she found life
happier there than it had been for her here she
returned, "Yes, I was glad to come," following
the statement with the little circle so often
used by the others. She, too, said that it
meant joy. We have since learned that it
means much more, but apparently they were
educating us by degrees. In this case the joy
was not hers alone, for the renewed communion
with her brought me great gladness.

Our friendship began long ago, in a Western
city, whither she had come in search of health.
Both were young, she a few years the elder.
She was alone. I never saw any member of
her family, and we had few friends in com-

mon, but between us, from the day we met, there was a strong bond of sympathy, which grew to deep affection, notwithstanding many differences between us. She was more widely read than I; I more actively in touch with life than she. She was a church woman; I was not. Her point of view was Eastern, mine at that time entirely Western. Our many disagreements were argued warmly and at length, but at bottom each knew that she could draw at will upon whatever strength or resource the other possessed, and the debt in the end was mine, when her death left a blank to which I could never be quite reconciled.

Her brief career seemed to contradict the law of compensation, upon which, until recently, my philosophy of life has been based. Meticulously truthful, scrupulous in all things, strong of purpose, giving of her best to life, life passed her by with a shrug. Keenly sensitive to beauty, whether spiritual, intellectual, or material, she was hampered in its pursuit by limited health and limited means. For years she struggled with uncongenial employment of one sort or another, denying herself the loaf she needed to procure the hyacinth she needed more. Longing for life at its fullest and richest, she scarcely touched its margin. Yearning for high peaks and wide outlook, she lived always on the plain. When, finally, the path seemed to be opening before her and she was pleasantly established, doing a healing and constructive work for which she was fitted, she died suddenly, still baffled, having given the last proof of her love for humanity by yielding her life for it, worn out by hard work, combating an epidemic in a college town.

Rejoiced to learn that at last she was happy, I asked whether she could tell us of her work, and she began, easily: "Yes, on the . . . on . . . on the. . . ." After long difficulty she accomplished it. "On the perpetual tour."

When she had verified this astonishing statement as correct, I suggested, "'Off ag'in, on ag'in, gone ag'in'?"

"That's it." For an eager spirit like Mary K.'s no happier heaven could be imagined.

Replying to further questions, she said that it was not just luck that I had caught her that first night. No, neither had she come to me from the other side of the world. "I've been working on you for a month," she said. "Ever since V—— was here." It was considerably more than a month, but time and place seem to have little significance to those on her plane.

Shortly after this Annie Manning interrupted again. It was said that Mary K. knew Annie Manning and wished me to find her brother. Inquiry developed the fact that he was the brother mentioned the first night I used planchette. His name was given as James Manning, and his address, Albany, New York. "United States Ho. . . ." We could not get beyond that. At one time the word seemed to be "Hotel." Unable to find any United States Hotel listed in Albany, I suggested Saratoga, but this was not accepted. Repeatedly asked to write to him, I could obtain no address.

Afterward the address was given as Albany, but not New York. Long efforts to write the name of the state resulted in "I . . .," ending in wavy lines. Suggestions of Illinois and Iowa brought negatives, but the mention of Indiana was greeted with a quick, "Yes." Vain and fatiguing efforts to get the rest of the address resulted in the indefinite "United States Ho . . ." and at last I gave it up, disappointed.

An hour later Annie Manning came again, but I asked her to let me talk to Mary K.

"Here! Mary K.," was the prompt response. "Do you remember all the good times?" I told her I did, and thought of them often. "All the many ae . . . an. . . ." There I lost it. She began it many times, in many ways, apparently trying to get a momentum that would carry her through. "All the many am . . . I mean ae . . . I meant to say anm. . . ." Too tired to continue, again I abandoned the attempt.

Annie Manning came once more, making futile efforts to give me her brother's address. She finally said it was "just United States Home." Once she wrote, "just Home." And once, "Honest, that's all."

I have never learned the whole truth about Annie Manning, who ceased, after the first fortnight, to manifest herself; whether because she lacked perseverance or because other influences were already at work, I do not know.

The next day I took up the pencil, expecting Mary Kendal, with news of her husband, but Mary K.'s strong, underlined signature greeted me instead. She said that Mr. Kendal was coming, adding: "On cen . . . cent. . . ."

"Century?" I suggested. "Twentieth Century Limited?"

"No . . . cen . . . ce . . . cent . . ." Finally, she agreed to Century—compromised on it, I learned later. Within five minutes a telegram came from Mr. Kendall—the first word I had received from him—saying that he would arrive in New York Sunday or Monday.

When I told him of this experience he exclaimed: "Central! New York Central!"

Which, for some reason, had not occurred to me. At the hour when Mary K. gave me this information he had ordered, at his club in Chicago, a ticket for the Lake Shore Limited— like the Twentieth Century, a New York Central train. Later, having the ticket actually in his possession, he telegraphed me that he would come by that train, reaching New York Sunday evening, but afterward changed to another road.

This second message arrived Saturday afternoon, and I at once inquired of Mary K. why she had said "Century." Instead of her familiar signature, however, "Frederick" was written.

Having ascertained that this was Frederick himself, and not a message about him, I asked him to go on.

"The Family are happy." At no time during this brief interview had I the slightest inkling of what was coming. As he had been always so courteous in acknowledgment, the first letters led me to think he was beginning his customary "Thank you." Saying that their happiness added greatly to my own, I asked if he had anything else to say.

"Yes. At your service. . . . At the next large family reunion you both will be present, won't you?"

I said we would try to be, and again he wrote his name, indicating that he had nothing more to say, whereupon I called Mary K., reproached her for inaccuracy, and asked why she had said Mansfield Kendal would come by the Century.

Apparently despairing of penetrating such density, she replied, merely: "He wanted to leave to-day." Later in the afternoon she said, "He will be perfectly ready to believe," which seemed to me highly improbable.

Some things written that afternoon came to my mind before they did to my fingers, and I asked whether she could not write the messages without first telling me what they were to be.

"Yes," she returned, "but it is harder for us and more exhausting for you." Weeks afterward, when this separate control of mind and pencil had been more fully demonstrated, it was more fully explained.

Remembering her statement that her work took her "on perpetual tour," I asked how long she would be here.

"I shall be near you for months," she said, and then began again her never wholly relinquished effort to write the message first attempted two days before. "Ao . . . an . . . aon . . . aem . . . aeons ago . . ."—here she made a frantic little joy circle—". . . we were lovers."

This surprised me, for it seemed unlike her

and was absolutely foreign to my thought, but when she had verified it, I asked: "Is reincarnation true, then?"

"No. Aeons ago . . . I was a friend of yours in ——." She mentioned a person whom I have known all my life. Again this seemed utter nonsense, but again she verified it. "We were concerned in being more and more curiously limited . . . more and more animal." Some of this came readily, some with halting and false starts, which—like Frederick—she crossed out herself.

At first this, too, seemed devoid of meaning, but after a little thought I asked whether she meant that we had been associated in some way as pure spirit.

"Everybody was pure spirit once, and will be again," was the rapid reply.

"Is this life a punishment, then?"

"No, a beginning of individuality."

"Does the individual continue to exist forever?"

"Yes."

"As pure spirit?"

"Yes."

"Then how were we associated as pure spirit?"

"We were the same purpose."

Completely puzzled, I asked, "Why do you say we were friends in ——?"

"He was the larger purpose, of which we were a part."

"The original purpose is not all the same, then?"

"No, there are many purposes in the beginning, but only one in the end."

"Does Frederick know all this?"

"All of it."

When she said good night, she added, "God bless you," and I asked: "Mary K., how do you see God? Frederick sees Him as light in dark places."

"Justice, light, progress."

"Is that God, or God's work?"

"Tested."

"You mean that you have tested it?"

"Yes."

The next day, Sunday—two weeks from the day she had first talked to me through planchette—she returned to this theme, which still seemed somewhat fantastic to my practical and pragmatical mind, with further allusions to our long association.

During the days of confusion and uncertainty before Mr. Kendal replied to my telegram, when his wife constantly implored me to write to him again, and I as constantly refused, insisting that she first show cause why she had misled me about his movements and whereabouts, I wrung from her an admission that in some way he had put her so far from him that she neither knew nor could learn anything about him, except that he suffered and needed her, which both Mary K. and Frederick verified. I said once to Mary K. that it was incredible that this could be, to which she laconically returned, "It can." After his actual receipt of my telegram, Mary Kendal never returned to me until she came with him, and the character of her earlier banishment, and consequent inability to perceive his movements, was still unexplained.

As the hour of his arrival approached I grew uneasy, and asked Mary K. whether he came happily or in dread.

"Certainly with o "—the joy circle, and as we have since learned, the circle of completion.

When I asked her to write it out in full to reassure me, the pencil ran back, underscoring "certainly." She said further that Mary Kendal was with him, and very happy.

"Has Mary Kendal been very unhappy?" I asked.

"No. Aeons ago they were one purpose."

"What has that to do with it?"

"She knew that he must answer if she could reach him."

"Does that hold good of evil purpose, too?"

"Yea."

VII

It seemed to me that if Mr. Kendal had not received my letters, and was in possession only of the meager information contained in my telegram, it was best that he should read the record of the earlier interviews with his wife before coming to communicate with her, and to that end the book containing the whole story was to be sent to his club before his arrival. Having decided this, it occurred to me to consult Mary K., who emphatically negatived the plan.

"No. Mary Kendal is most anxious to tell him herself now." She told us to make brief explanations, adding: "All he needs now is Mary Kendal."

Shortly afterward Mary K.'s now familiar summons—an indescribable sensation in the arm or hand—recalled me to the pencil, and she wrote, quickly and firmly: "Mary Kendal wants you to change your record."

Surprised, I asked what change she wished, and was told to take out everything relating to her banishment from Mansfield's life, because she preferred to tell him that in her own way.

"Shall I show him the record at all?" I asked.

"Yes, but take that out first." Fortunately, the record is kept in a loose-leaf, typewritten book, so this was not difficult.

As the day wore on I grew more and more nervous. Suppose he should be more hurt than helped? Suppose we should fail? Rarely in my life have I dreaded anything so much, or felt so little confidence in anything I had deliberately undertaken to do. By nine o'clock I was in a nervous chill. Meanwhile Mr. Kendal telephoned that he had found my letters, which had been returned to his club, and that he would join us presently.

Upon his arrival he told us that he had been one of the early members of the Society for Psychical Research in this country, and had spent several years investigating phenomena of this nature, together with various other young men, under the general supervision of Prof. William James, Dr. Minot Savage, and others of that group. He mentioned some of the frauds and self-deceptions uncovered at that time, but said he believed the ultimate conclusion to have been that there were certain well-authenticated phenomena for which no logical or scientific explanation had been found.

Nothing that he said, however, indicated to the slightest degree his attitude toward the question in hand, and I received an impression that his mood was critical, which steadied me. The disappointment, should we fail, would be less hideous. In the end, he suggested a trial, and after preparing the table, Cass left us alone.

The pencil started almost immediately, with a strange, jerkily rhythmical movement—due possibly to Mary's agitation, possibly to mine, but wrote very distinctly, without pause or faltering. It was evident at once that the message conveyed more to him than its words suggested.

Much later in the evening he told me that for some time after Mary left him he had believed that if she still existed anywhere in the universe she would contrive somehow to let him know; but as months had passed into years, with no sign from her, while never entirely losing faith in the continued integrity of the individual after death, his despair had deepened with his growing conviction that "the drop that was Mary" had been swept on in the stream and forever lost to him. Widely read in philosophies and unable to forget them, steeped—despite his practical occupation—in scientific and intellectual theory, he had feared to rely upon a reunion in a future of which no proof had been given him, lest he be grounding his faith in the sands of his own hope.

It was to this unhappy conviction—a conviction so strong in its negation that for a time she had been unable to penetrate in any way the psychic atmosphere it created—that she addressed herself in those first written lines. She used, also, her intimate name for him, which I had never heard, and his for her, which I knew, although I supposed the peculiar spelling used on this occasion to be an error, until he told me otherwise.

He asked one or two questions about personal matters, which I assumed to be in the nature of tests, which she answered briefly, though not very specifically, concluding: "I cannot tell you anything to-night, except that I am so happy. I had lost you, and you are found again. Let me talk to you to-morrow."

Some time later he wanted to know why he could not read her mind direct, and she replied: "You can, in time, if you will let me in, and learn. We can have such communion as we never had before, because one veil is now removed. But that will take time to learn. It is true. It can be. . . . Take me into your heart and soul joyfully, without resentment or grief, and you will soon learn to read my thoughts as I have read yours since I seemed to leave you.

"Then I can tell you things that I cannot say through any messenger. . . . You can learn. . . . All I want now is to convince you that I am alive and longing to be with you and to have communication directly with you. It is impossible for me to do that alone. But I had to reach you somehow, and Margaret was the first way I found."

We talked a little of the possibility of his establishing direct communication with her. I asked whether he could use a pencil in this way, and she returned: "Yes, if he will try every day, he could in time, I think. There is always a way for us to reach our dearest ones, if they only persevere."

During a pause, with the pencil-point still resting on the paper, I told him of Mary K.'s assertion that eons ago some of us had been one and that we still continue one in purpose. Mary Kendal took it up immediately.

"Manzie, you and I are the same purpose. That is the reason that, once reunited, we cannot be separated, except by our deliberate yielding to a different and disintegrating purpose. That is the eternal battle—between the purposes of progress and building and the purposes of disintegration. It goes on in your life, and it goes on less bitterly in ours. Help me build, as we began, toward the great unity. . . . All of us here are working against those forces of disintegration so rife in your life now, and every bit of retention of unity that is for upbuilding helps us and helps the great purpose for which we work. . . . You and I began working for that long ago, and each of us will always continue to work for it. But we shall be happier if we do it consciously together. . . . Don't think of me as far away. . . . We will welcome to our unity anything or anybody who strengthens the purpose, but let us always hold fast to each other."

Here was the first actual statement, however brief and incomplete, of that theory of life which seems—to us who received it first, at least—so rational, and so full of inspiration and hope.

Referring to her phrase, "all of us here," he asked: "Is 'here' a place, or a state, or both?"

"Both," she answered, quickly. "It is the beginning of eternal life." After a moment, she added: "The state is fluid; the place is ephemeral."

"I believe it!" he exclaimed. "That's more nearly an explanation than anything I ever heard before."

78

"This is more nearly the truth than anything you ever heard before. That's why. . . . Truth in your life is comparative. Here it is absolute, but not dogmatic."

. He said that she had not been given to the use of a philosophic vocabulary in this life, and must have acquired it there, to which, at the moment, she made no response.

Some time after Cass rejoined us Mr. Kendal asked how much farther, or how much more clearly, they could see about purely business or political matters than we.

"We can see much farther, but we are not permitted to tell you, except by ethical suggestion. Part of your development comes through your struggle to decide, and while we see your struggle, we can help only by giving you as much of our strength and light as you can take. It is a moral universe, Manzie." The underscoring is hers. ·

Out of his wide experience with psychic phenomena, he gave me much comfort regarding the inaccuracies and misleading statements that had so greatly disquieted me. He argued that these discrepancies might easily be caused by some factor or factors unknown to us, operating on another plane, and was entirely untroubled by them. In this connection, Mary K. said to me the next day: "We regard things successfully started as accomplished."

[Some weeks later Mr. Kendal suggested another possible reason for these apparent inaccuracies, using as a comparison a familiar experiment in physics. He reminded us that if a rod be projected in a straight line between the eye and a coin at the bottom of a bowl of water, its tip will miss the coin by a distance varying with the angle of vision and the depth of the water. Assuming that the difference between this plane and the next must be vastly greater than that between air and water, he argued that there might be a factor comparable to this deflection of ray influencing their perception of material, specific details of this plane—a simile which Mary K. subsequently characterized as "almost perfect."]

It was three o'clock in the morning when Mr. Kendal left us to return to his club—but he went convinced. Like Mrs. Gaylord, his confidence was inspired not only by the temper and tenor of the messages he had received, but by the accompanying consciousness of a familiar personality, akin to the certainty of identity one feels in talking to a friend by telephone or in reading a characteristic letter. Like her, too, he said that in several instances his unspoken thought had been directly answered.

The next day we resumed our conversation
—for it amounted to that—with Mary.

"There will be hours, and sometimes days,
when you cannot feel me, just at first," she
warned him. "But I beg of you, do not let
the doubts prevail. I shall be there, unless
that disintegrating force drives me away.
That's a power we here cannot fight alone.
Faith is not the desire to believe, as some men
have said. It is the thread that connects
your life and ours, and when it is broken we
are powerless to reach you."

We spoke again of inaccuracies concerning
mundane activities, and he elaborated somewhat his theory that it is unwise to ask and
unsafe to rely upon answers about concrete,
specific things, because in translating them into
terms of our plane we are apt to overlook some
transforming, unknown factor, and so go wrong.

"Besides that," Mary took up the discussion,
"you must work out your problem yourself.
We can only help you definitely and directly
in the larger things that pertain to the life of
our purpose. Your present problem may be
solved in any of several ways, and will perhaps affect the ephemeral part of your life.
Your greater concern, and my only concern,
is with the fluid part, which we shall share
together always, now."

He asked, after some further talk, whether there was danger of my being exploited or employed by malign influences—a suggestion entirely new to me—to which she replied in the negative, adding: "Trust us for that. Her own purpose is definite, and with that foundation, we can protect her fully." Apparently she underestimated the strength of the enemy, or perhaps she merely disregarded the temporary confusion created by occasional sorties.

Thinking that he might know something about New Albany, Indiana, I told him of the Annie Manning episode and my failure to ascertain her brother's address. Our conversation was interrupted by an unsigned statement that the brother was not in New Albany, Indiana, but in Albany, New Hampshire, flatly contradicting a previous statement. My impatient comment was answered by an assurance that Annie Manning had recently passed to the next plane and was confused. A suggestion that possibly Annie Manning was one of the malign forces mentioned brought no response, unless Mary Kendal's next words constituted an indirect reply.

"Manzie dear, . . . you will have entirely different forces working against you, from those trying to control Margaret, but we will truly and surely protect you both."

Again, following a period of silence, she wrote a brisk reply to his unspoken thought, adding, when he commented upon it: "You see, I do know what is in your mind, and the time may not be far away when you can read mine as clearly. I don't always answer your thought, because Margaret has still some fear of being deceived in her reception of my message, and it is hard, but as she works with us she will learn unconsciously to yield, just as you will learn to detect my presence."

"Is there anything I can do to help you or your work?" he asked. "Or must it be all take and no give with us?"

I have no record of her reply. She began by saying that any actively constructive effort here helped them there, because it helped the great purpose. This was followed by a message so intimately and exquisitely his that I felt it almost a desecration to be the messenger through whom it necessarily came. He took that part of the roll away with him, and I am glad to say that twenty-four hours later no word of it remained in my memory. It was truly his.

The next night he came again, very happily. She, too, was in a lightsome mood, and while there was some serious talk, most of it was pure effervescence, frequently witty, sometimes brilliant. Unfortunately, little of this may be quoted, either because of its too personal character or because, like much amusing conversation, it was too essentially of the mood and the moment to bear translation into type.

Constantly he exclaimed at the characteristic quality of her repartee, to my great surprise. I said that I had never seen this merry side of her, and had not dreamed that it existed, to which she replied: "You never saw us when we were not in trouble—before."

"Let me in and don't chafe," she told him, in one of her more serious moments, "and I can tell you much of what I see ahead. Grief, resentment, bitterness and doubt are our highest barriers. There is no cause for grief in a relation closer than your life there knows. There is no ground for resentment in the price we pay. There can be no bitterness in growth and development together—quicker growth, fuller development, than could be possible if one of us were not here. It is largely in the point of view, this thing that is called grief."

In the course of their drifting talk he asked her how to go about starting persons who have no starting-point—"no peg to hang things on."

"Sometimes a bomb is effective. But the fragments are not always efficient." We laughed, and she added: "They just have to wait and grow up, Manzie dear. We learn here that our frantic haste there has been foolish. Growth must take its own time. . . . No, I didn't!" I had called attention to her failure to cross a t, and she returned to it with a flourish. Several times thereafter she made a little joke by conspicuously dotting her i's.

In the midst of one ecstatic whirl she paused to inquire: "Who ever started the foolish notion that there was no life beyond that one? Was he a philosopher, or a dyspeptic, or both?" And again, following some amusing nonsense, "You don't think this would sound trivial to a scientific investigator, do you?"

"What's the matter with the scientific type of mind?" he asked.

"Mostly it's pure intellect—and life isn't."

During another moment of jesting he said: "I don't think I'll bother to walk home. I'll just float."

"Come on! We'll float together," she retorted. "Do you raise that, or call?"

Laughing, he returned: "I'll pass the buck to Saint Peter," whereupon she intimated that Saint Peter was not immediately available.

"Who hold the keys?"

"You hold your own—not transferable."

"You are mostly pure idealist," was another comment, a little later, replying to something he said about his own attitude toward life, "and got lost for a while in the dark." He began to say that he should hardly have called himself an idealist, but already she was answering. "A true idealist is not a man who limits life to ideas, but a man who puts his ideals into life."

One otherwise serious statement, concerning the influence of "hard-headed, intelligent men who are not afraid to testify to their faith" in these revelations, was given a humorous touch by the signature, "Missionary Mary."

"Do you want me to go forth and testify, also?" I asked.

"No, you do it, and that involves too much," she replied. "Let your converts testify. You go on playing hermit."

"Have you seen William James?" he asked.

"He is instructing many of us. Some of my newly acquired vocabulary he taught me. He is more certain and less philosophical than he was. The will to believe has given way to the duty of faith. He has learned more quickly than most do, because he is truly sincere and had cultivated his ground well. Now he is still a leader of thought and accomplishment, but his instruction is dynamic. . . . He is a very fine force, Manzie, and is doing magnificent work here, but he no longer smothers it in language."

Much of this parting interview must be omitted.

At nine o'clock Sunday night Mr. Kendal had approached this experience in a state of high nervous tension. At midnight on Tuesday, fifty-one hours later, he left us to return home, imbued, like Mrs. Gaylord, with the vitalizing quality of this touch with the unseen and carrying with him the happy conviction that he did not go alone.

VIII

Up to this time the messages, while frequently impersonal in tenor, had seemed entirely personal in direction. It happened, fortunately, that both Mrs. Gaylord and Mr. Kendal were more interested in the wide meaning and purpose of life than in the narrow, individual details of its conduct, and to that interest chiefly those nearest them on the next plane had addressed themselves. The rapidity with which these communications came, and their surprising volume, was attributed to the fact that in both cases the time in which they could be given through me was limited.

Aside from the attendant nervous strain— which has been less, on the whole, than one would expect, probably because these efforts have been followed by such sound and refreshing sleep as I had not known before in years— the manual labor involved in taking these long messages, and in typewriting them afterward, has been excessive. Assuming, however, that this flood of disclosure would be diminished when the necessity for immediate expression passed, I looked forward to leisure and opportunity for some long talks with Mary K., which should be more detailed and personal than our somewhat fragmentary intercourse thus far had been.

This was briefly delayed by requests to establish interplane communication for one or two other friends, whose need was more imperative than my own, when significant and beautiful messages—not to be quoted here— were obtained. One of these slightly elaborated the now familiar idea of the close and intimate relation of certain persons to one another, because of their union in a common and eternal purpose. In a letter to Mr. Kendal I mentioned this, adding: "It begins to look like a gospel, doesn't it?"

Finally, however, my own opportunity came, on Thursday, March 21st, but instead of permitting me to propound any of the many questions I had in mind, Mary K. delivered a detailed message of instruction that left me astounded and incredulous. Most of this is too personal to repeat, but some of it must be quoted, in view of what followed.

"... We have much to tell, and few through whom to tell it. You have the sensitiveness to receive and the power to convince. When you

have fully grasped the meaning of what we
have to tell, you must make it known, but not
before we give you the whole of it. You will
get the truth slowly, through helping many
people, but keep the full knowledge frankly
back until it is all told. . . . Let them know
you are withholding it, but do not let them
have it in fragments."

"You mean they are not to be told of the
division of original purpose into individual
life?"

"No, they must have that to build on. But
there will be more given to you in fragments.
Piece it together for yourself, but do not give
it to any one as long as you are still receiving
it. . . . The light is breaking, and you are the
aees . . . accustomed . . ."—later she returned,
to write "accredited" over this word. I think
neither was what she tried for. Perhaps ac-
cessible?—". . . force to make the meaning
clear. . . . It is what we have long sought and
just found. That is the reason we are giving
you things never told before. You are to
pass them on when the time comes. . . . This
is your work, your contribution to the great
purpose, which will be revealed to you little
by little. Keep clear of disturbing contacts,
as you have done, and keep your purpose true.
You have already recognized this as a gospel.

It is more. It is a faith. Be true to it and it will save many from suffering. That is the reason I am here now and shall remain. I am the force used by greater forces to reach the world through you. We have always been the same purpose, and I can reach you freely." After an allusion to mental purpose, she defined it thus: "Mental purpose is the force that convinces men. Moral purpose is that which persuades them. We prefer conviction. It lasts, where persuasion fades. Nothing more now, but this is only the beginning. Mary K."

After the first phrase, save for one or two brief pauses, this long communication was so rapidly written that I could not follow it with my left hand, though I made several attempts, as my right arm became greatly fatigued. At no time had I the slightest impression of what was to be said, and during most of it I was too bewildered to think clearly, my mind being filled with blank wonder and vague questioning, scarcely formulated, yet immediately answered.

The next day she resumed her exhortation.

". . . This is war work. It is going to make the war seem what it is, a reawakening of the souls of men. There is no higher duty than to make a man know his own soul and the souls of his fellows. The war will be justified only if this result is obtained. We work for that here, and we ask you to help us. There can be no victory unless this is accomplished. . . . Be true to your purpose and ours, and help us build for light and progress, against the forces of doubt and disintegration."

To an inquiry about Germany, apropos of her mention of the war, she replied: "Germany is the united purpose of fear. It is her weapon and her weakness, and it is to defeat the force she symbolizes that we all work. . . . There you have the real war, the battle that has gone on from the beginning. This is one of the crises of eternity."

Here I thought of certain past wars, when the victorious barbarians set civilization back.

"Sometimes the forces of disintegration have won, sometimes we. But their victory is never permanent, because they are negative and we are positive. They delay us, but we live and work. We shall win in the end, but that is far away. We call you to fight with the forces of life and light. You can do more with us than you can alone."

The following day found me still incredulous, and she said:

". . . Tell them that you are doing the

people's work, under secret orders, and that they will perhaps know presently what it is. They will all recognize it when it is given to them, except those souls not mentally free from fear."

From this she passed immediately into the first of that remarkable series of communications which she has called Lessons. Again the writing was so rapid that my arm ached to the shoulder, long before she had finished, from the incessant movement to and fro across the table, and again my mind was filled with blank amazement.

Perhaps it should be stated that, although I have written more or less light fiction during the past fifteen years, literary composition is to me a slow and laborious exercise. Especially is this true of opening paragraphs, which generally require many hours of work. Unfortunately, the time consumed in writing one of these Lessons was never noted, but with one or two exceptions, when I was too tired to receive readily, they were done without hesitation and with extraordinary rapidity. Also, while in personal messages the mental impression is sometimes given to me a little before the physical movement occurs, never during the writing of the Lessons had I the slightest inkling of what was to follow. One

by one the words were revealed by the moving
pencil, my principal sensations being wonder
and incredulity. Until frequent repetition had
accustomed me to this experience, I felt as if
I must be dreaming.

Part II

THE LESSONS

"The lessons came from great forces combined. They represent unity of all purposes, and were framed by the co-operation and agreement of the greatest forces of each constructive purpose, to reach the consciousness of men in general terms of your plane."

I

"ALL pure purpose is fearless, whether for good or evil, but few humans are pure purpose, and the first fight is in themselves. All this has been said before in effect, but based on other premises. This is the first time the original purpose has been defined and explained. For centuries men have sought the source of life. This is the first time they have been ready to accept the whole truth about that, or to be prepared for the next step.

"Once convinced that chaos grew from purposes born of the Force Beyond Perfection, purposes perfect from the beginning, but at war because they contained within themselves all the elements of life and of conflict—once convinced of this, men will gradually find their own clear purposes defined, and the war within themselves will cease. They will choose definitely to build or to destroy, to be honest or dishonest. Self-deception will be less easy or possible, and the fight will then be with you, as it is now with us, between forces clearly indicated. Now you are all confused by a war within a war, infinitely continued. Conflict multiplied by the number of purposes in each purpose. This has been recognized, but the remedy has never been clearly found. It lies in the conviction that force of every nature is purpose, which has existed from the beginning, and that the force which builds is beneficent and may be clearly segregated and united.

"The Force Beyond Perfection is composed of all things, and therefore understands all things. The original purposes were all good, and will be again, if they can all become intelligent. They became evil through attraction of like for like, akin to your atomic attraction, and chaos resulted. This struggle created a desire and determination to exist in concrete form, to add a new force to the forces of chaos. That was a great conflict, resulting in a tie. Purposes became fused in the same individual, and the battle infinitely multiplied, but yet not lost. Now the effort of both participants is for united purpose again, and the fusion of purposes in each individual makes the confusion greater and the fight more bitter. Men are swayed first by one purpose and then by another, and are themselves unable to distinguish between good and evil.

"This precipitated the Great War with you, the purposes in the Central Empires being more nearly united than elsewhere. Their purposes are fundamentally destructive, because . fundamentally autocratic, based on fear, and would ultimately reduce civilization to infancy again. The reason Germany has been able to fight so long is because her purpose is conscious, while the Allies fight blindly but determinedly, moved by purposes they do not recognize and yet must obey. They talk of unity, but do not perceive its nature. They are misled by phrases hollow, but plausible, and do not perceive them to be the enemy in disguise— not the mortal enemy, but the ancient purpose, divided into many.

"The light is beginning to break now, and the hour has almost come for the forces of construction to unite and smite powerfully. But it must be consciously, as the purpose of construction, if the victory is to be permanent or truly for progress. Men must learn to choose their purposes consciously and intelligently, to be definitely and actually building for a definite and actual future. There is too much quarreling about ways and means, and too little recognition of the goal. Too much self, and too little sympathy. This is equally true of all classes of society. Materialism has been rank in the tenement and in the cottage, as in palace and counting-room.

"It is a common purpose we serve, for building or for tearing down. It is impossible to be consistently for both continuously. That has made the Great War, and that is the struggle that must be settled in the minds of men before there can be peace on earth or lasting and progressive brotherhood.

"This is the first lesson."

II

"THIS is the second lesson.

"The forces of disintegration are gathering for a titanic struggle, of which your Great War is only the beginning. Had Germany won there, they would have a foothold with you that we would find it difficult, if not impossible, to combat effectively for many years. The spirits of free men would have been soiled with fear and despair, and the forces of doubt and disintegration would have held civilization captive.

"Germany has felt her forces weaken and fail under the onslaught of freedom, light, and progress, and the forces of disintegration are deserting her. She is left alone, to work her way, through mazes of despair, back to a place in the sun. She must find her own way. She chose to follow the forces of destruction, and they will surely destroy her.

"But the forces she followed are uniting for a fiercer fight, more subtle, more deadly, more furious. Hidden beneath the garments of peace and good will, they make ready to poison the minds of men before destroying their forces and delaying their purposes.

"This is the battle to which we call you and all who are for progress. This is the message you are to give the world, to warn them of the danger at hand. The time has come when men must choose consciously to fight for or against the forces of construction. They are confused from the conflict within themselves, running hither and thither, calling for help from the gods they have made unto themselves, but looking only to the present good, perceiving only the present purpose, fearing only the present defeat. They will find no help from these gods, for they have impotent feet of clay.

"The forces of disintegration have made friends with the poor and the needy, and have fed them husks of brotherhood. They have made friends with the powerful and rich, and have tempted them with earth and its kingdoms. They have fed the artist falsehoods, and the writer fear of fear. They have touched the priest with tainted hands, and rulers with fear of the people. They have entered the home and rent it asunder, and the temple is a market-place. These are the works of the purposes we fight, and thus do they disguise themselves. Unless this can be brought home to the souls of men, the fight will be long and bitter.

"Forget the class and remember the man. Forget the price and remember the pearl. Forget the labor and remember the fruit. Forget the temple and remember God.

"Men fight together for one end alone—the purpose for which they live. It is hard to find there, in the confusion of personal conflict, but the time is at hand when it must be found.

"The forces of light are positive. Shun negation. The forces of freedom are individual. Shun dependence. The forces of progress are fearless. Shun fearful combinations. Work together as individuals, consciously cooperating, not as sheep. You will learn to think. You will learn to feel. You will learn to see. Then we may move on to the next phase of development toward the great purpose.

"The forces of disintegration are wily, but fearful. Bullies and cowards. But when they are united in sufficiently strong numbers, fearless and unscrupulous. They fear the reawakening of the forces of progress in your life. This is the reason they gather now, to smite while the world is weary. Disguised as purposes of light, they hope for welcome.

"This is our call to arms. Arouse ye! Come forth for freedom, light, justice, and progress—consciously, freely, strongly.

"This is the second lesson."

III

"THIS is the third lesson.

"When men learn that the Force Beyond Perfection is purpose, which has personified itself in them, they will grow to feel the possibilities to which they have heretofore been insensible.

"Life is purpose. Purpose is force. Force is personality, from highest to lowest, from saint to stick and stone. Men have called it many things, but what it is none have perceived clearly.

"Eternal purpose is perfect justice, perfect fearlessness, perfect understanding, perfect honesty, perfect sympathy, perfect unity, and eternal growth, which is progress perfectly expressed. This is the end for which we work. Not Nirvana. Not oblivion. Not power stagnant and powerless. But a perfect balance, progressing to purposes and powers as yet undreamed. This is the Eternal Purpose, toward which all purpose moves. Purposes of construction consciously and determinedly, purposes of destruction unwillingly and inevitably. They fear us, they fight us, they seek to destroy us, not perceiving that they must in the end rejoin us, having left us in the beginning.

"To bring this home to the souls of men is our first duty, and for that reason those of us nearest to your life work first among men. Purpose frees forces you but dimly apprehend, and free forces construct a foundation in your life for the perfect unity of Eternal Purpose.

"Any force not free destroys itself. Any good not animated and active destroys itself. Force imprisoned becomes destruction. Good imprisoned becomes evil. All are fundamentally good, fundamentally beneficent, but have become powers for destruction through lack of progressive development and exercise.

"All men are fusions of many purposes, moved by many forces, answering to many calls. Each responds to the call of his dominant purpose, which flows and fluctuates with his life's struggle. One day he destroys, and cares not. One day he builds, and marvels at his power. One day he sleeps and forgets. One day he fights to the death for a purpose he had not yesterday, and loses to-morrow. This is the life of man, and this our field of battle. There are other lives, other struggles, other lessons to learn, but this is the first.

"Purpose manifests itself in man inevitably in action. His purpose is not what he believes, not what he desires, but what he is and does. If he destroys, and builds not on the ruins, he is against us. If he falls and fails not, he is with us, though he stumble an hundred times. He fights within himself the ancient fight, and if he win that, his eternal battle is won. Thereafter, he is part and parcel of the forces of construction.

"Purpose answers freely only to its kind, freely and fearlessly it responds to the call of self. If a man be captive to destructive forces, he responds to the cry, Destroy! But if he be given to powers of progress, he builds, though his eyes be blinded and his hands cut off.

"In every man captive to forces of disintegration the builder lies dormant. To reach that faint glow of Eternal Purpose is the first duty of every constructive force. Call to it, rouse it, free it, and it will eventually respond. But do not smother it with false charity, darken it by conflicting precepts, weaken it by fictitious aid. Every individual must serve his own purpose. Only thus is the integrity of the whole conserved. Though he be only a doorkeeper in the house of the Lord, yet does he

serve his eternal purpose as truly as the priest.
Let each man learn his purpose and serve
forcefully where his development has placed
him. Only thus can he progress.

"Purposes are divided. Thus do they show
themselves to men. The purpose of Progress
is first and greatest, because it moves all the
others toward the Great Purpose. The other
constructive purposes are these, divided and
subdivided: Light, Justice, Truth, Production,
Healing, Building. Each divided and divisible
by any of the others, yet pure and perfect in
itself. Light may dwell with Healing or Production, but only Light calls unto Light, only
Justice unto Justice.

"All forces of construction work together,
yet each purpose separate unto itself. Choose
ye, therefore. Build or tear down, produce or
destroy, illumine or obscure, free men, or hold
them captive to themselves. Choose daily and
hourly the purpose ye serve.

"This is the third lesson."

IV

"THIS is the fourth lesson.

"The world fears purpose that is free and fearless. All the forces of humanity are turned against freedom. The church imposes its creed, the class imposes its caste, the profession imposes its etiquette, the moralist imposes his fear, the libertine imposes his folly. All men are bound by the conventions of church, caste, profession, or moral status. Thus do they throw wide the door to forces of disintegration. Each man assumes a purpose not his own; a force that is his own deserts him.

"Free development demands free purpose and concentrated force. Wherever two or three are gathered together to follow the same purpose in free and conscious co-operation, there force is multiplied. Wherever an hundred are assembled to be led like sheep by the bell-wether, there force is debauched and disintegrated.

"Because men have huddled together in

fear, destruction threatens them. Because free speech has been debauched to fell purpose, free men distrust it. Men, forces of disintegration, but possessed of glib tongues, have played bell-wether to the multitude. Priests of purpose, whose counsel was inspired by the Eternal, have been thrust aside and stoned. Better were it for the immortal man to follow his purpose to death and mortal oblivion, than to lose ·his force to the bell-wether. Many purposes make great purpose. Many · forces unite for freedom. But better for immortal man to destroy greatly and greatly strive than to sink his purpose in the medley disguised as brotherhood.

"A great brotherhood is possible only when its component parts are great. Strength lies not in numbers, but in purpose. The fit may not lie down with the unfit, and their progeny survive. The strong may not yield their purpose to the weak, and their force remain.

"A light breaks in the East—Russia, given as a sacrifice to the brotherhood of men. A light not of star or dawn, but of sacrificial fire. Heed it, guard it, ye youths and virgins, for by its flaming sacrifice are ye saved.

"Brotherhood is purpose of progress, not purpose of profit. Brotherhood is made beautiful by unity, not by schism. Brotherhood suffereth long, and is kind. Brotherhood regardeth every brother, great and small. Brotherhood waiteth upon brother and grumbleth not. All build together the common home of all.

"Seek ye those of your own purpose. Unite together all who fain would build. Master and man, architect and mason, financier and farm laborer, all work to the same end, and this is Brotherhood.

"To work for the same purpose, in whatever capacity may be necessary, this is the only true Brotherhood.

"This is the fourth lesson."

V

"THIS is the fifth lesson.

"Men have long cherished the ideal of
Brotherhood, but they have clung to the letter
of the ancient law and lost its spirit. Before
the days of liberty, when men were languishing
in slavery or bound as vassals, sell all thou
hast and give to the poor had a significance
lost in a day of free labor and industrial progress. The spirit of the law is unchanged and
unchangeable, but the letter progresses with
civilization's advance.

"To-day, the first essential of brotherhood
is freedom. Freedom to think, freedom to believe, freedom to strive, freedom to develop,
from highest to lowest. And the employer who
refuses this opportunity to the men who work
under him is no more truly a force for disintegration than the laborer who refuses to co-
operate with his employer and thus proves
himself unworthy of a place in the procession
of progress.

"There can be no house that will stand against storm that has not foundation, walls, and roof. There can be no society that will withstand disintegration that has not labor, capital, and market. When capital oppresses labor, forces of disintegration are freed. When labor dominates capital, forces of disintegration are freed. When the people forget justice, forces of disintegration are freed. And the destruction of one is the destruction of all. The rich man who denies his brother freedom is a destroyer. The poor man who denies his brother freedom is a destroyer in no less degree. Each is a part of the other, and each follows eternal purpose to one end—construction and progress.

"The man who has freedom of thought, freedom of purpose, freedom of action, is free, though he be a pauper, and is free to choose whether he will build or destroy. The man who is bound by any tie that dictates his thought, belief, or action is a force of disintegration, because he may not follow his purpose freely and with all his force. The man who has freedom and wealth, and forgets his brother, is a force of disintegration. The man who has strength and poverty, and forgets his brother, is a force of disintegration. Equality of opportunity does not demand or imply equality of development. Many men are rich who use their wealth to forward the purposes of construction. Many there are who waste it and invite disintegration. Many men are poor, who use their strength to help along construction. They are forces of progress, and will find their places here. Many there are who delay the march, and invite disintegration. What shall it profit a man, though he gain the earth, if he lose his own soul?

"There are seven purposes. Progress, Light, Truth, Healing, Building, Production, and Justice. Equally great, save Progress, which moves them all. One of these must each man serve, if he proceeds toward the Great Purpose. Whether great or small, high or low, wise or foolish, learned or ignorant, rich or poor, powerful or apparently impotent, each human individual is a force for construction or for disintegration, and follows his purpose to its inevitable end: constructive forces to construction of great purposes, disintegrating forces to the long struggle that can have but one end, however distant—construction.

"There are many phases of development, each looking onward to the next If a man climb without envy, forgetting himself in his purpose, he shall climb far. If he look with envy at his higher brother and with scorn at those below him, he shall climb on slipping sands and find himself again at the foot.

"Bear ye one another's burdens is a command unchanged and unchangeable. Give unto each his opportunity to grow, and to build for progress. Freedom to strive is the one right inherent in existence, the strong and the weak each following his own purpose, with all his force, to the one great end. And he who binds or limits his brother's purpose binds himself now and hereafter. But he who extends his brother's opportunity builds for eternity.

"Choose ye.

"This is the fifth lesson."

VI

"THIS is the sixth lesson.

"Men are afraid of fear. They fear to fear, and fall into folly. Fear of disintegrating purposes makes for wisdom, and wisdom makes for construction. Fear is a disintegrating force made constructive, when directed against disintegration.

"Wisdom in high places has been dethroned, and intellectual curiosity usurps the scepter. Men who should lay foundations of wisdom experiment with fantasies of the intellectual dreamer.

"Brotherhood, to one class, is a defensive organization, for protection. Brotherhood, to another class, is an offensive organization, for pillage. Brotherhood, to another class, is an organized attempt to preserve the unfit. Brotherhood, to another class, is a dream of unorganized following of untried theories. None of these know that all men are brothers.

"Evolution of matter follows evolution of

116

purpose, but when material things are left behind, purpose continues to progress. Why, then, lose your purpose in pursuit of material gain?

"Church and state alike urge morality for personal ends, and recommend personal punishments. There is no morality. There is only purpose, constructive or destructive. There is no punishment. There is only consequence.

"Personal motives are deterrent forces, neither actively constructive nor actively destructive, except as they may be applied. These forces crowd in between the contending purposes, hindering both and helping neither, except when compelled by sheer force of numbers to sweep on with one or the other.

"Forces of disintegration are frequently mistaken for personal motives. They are always destructive. Personal motives are always deterrent. Self-interest excludes sympathy. Purpose demands sympathy. Self-interest excludes true unity. Unity is the Great Purpose. Any morality based on personal interest is, therefore, a deterrent force.

"The time has not yet come when men in the mass have vision. The great Purpose to the small mind is vague and of no significance. Personal motives are more easily recognized than purpose, and Church and state emphasize and encourage them. But the time is at hand when great conflicting purposes will meet in combat for control of men. Wake the sleepers. Cast off little things. Sink personal motives. Rouse Church and state to perception of force and purpose, and unite together, regardless of class, creed, or party, to win the world to purposes of construction.

"Church and state urge unity, and yield none. Tolerance, freedom, fearlessness, light —these are almost strangers to temple or court. Little by little the lines are softening. Little by little we gain on fear. Here a tolerant and noble clergyman, there a statesman who serves the state. But for one of these, a thousand huddle under creed or slogan, and fear of freedom impels them all. This is because they have not recognized purpose, and they impede progress who might be its power.

"Come forth, then, priests, teachers, and leaders! Call upon the people, not to follow, not to huddle, not to hesitate, but to choose. Set ye the seven purposes clearly before them, clearly perceiving them, ye that call, and bid them choose, for the life of all, the purpose they will serve.

"Thus may deterrent forces become constructive, and the Great Purpose known of all men.

"This is the sixth lesson."

VII

"THIS is the seventh lesson.

"Before the light of freedom dawned on the world, a puissant chaos of purposes and forces fought for control of the liberties of men. A short space of time brought liberty of body, after the perception of the people had been clarified by the gradual development of the ideal of liberty. They moved rapidly toward it, when they began to understand it, with halts and hesitations and blunders, but forcefully and inevitably still. They overthrew kings and barons, and took into their own hands the physical and material government of their kind. But their minds and forces are still enslaved and shackled by outworn tradition. Onward Christian soldiers, is a plea for progress; but it has become a recessional, not a marching song. Men have made their justice vassal to tradition, and their brotherhood fief to gain.

"Men have learned the value of free bodies,

but free force, mental or spiritual, terrifies and puzzles them still. They have learned to discipline their bodies, to keep them strong and clean. But they fear to trust the purposes and forces, without chains and prison bars to hold them, lest they make chaos of civilization. Church, state, profession, trade, guild, or society commands: Thou shalt not think. Follow, yield, accept, and endure, but let not thought be found among ye, lest the bars be broken and destruction loosed.

"Many men follow; a few men think. These are the overlords, the kings and barons of forces that might be free. But freedom demands free purpose, and fre purpose demands justice

"No man is free who commands not himself. No man is free who forgets his brother. No man is free who fears to follow his own purpose with all his force. No man is free who fails to carry his share of the common load. He may have wealth and luxury; yet is he slave. He may be tempted by beauty; yet is he slave. He may be frightened by calamity; yet is he slave. He may be beaten by strangers; yet is he slave. No man is free who commands not himself in any emergency. He may lose wealth and luxury, and still be free. He may dwell with squalor, who loves beauty, and still be free. He may be defrauded by his brother, and still be free. He may be shackled by strangers, beaten and imprisoned, and still be free.

"Freedom lieth not in a man's estate, but in the man himself.

"This is the seventh lesson."

VIII

"This is the eighth lesson.

"Many men try to perceive the purpose of God in truth and beauty and justice, and fail to recognize that the Eternal Purpose is unlimited by the detached conceptions of men. Truth is one of the fundamental purposes. Beauty is a subdivision of Building. Justice is fundamental. All are part of the Eternal Purpose. But the Great Purpose is unity.

"The fundamental purposes are common to all men, of whatever race, color, belief, or prejudice. They are the foundation from which the forces of Eternal Purpose start, and by their divisions only are men ultimately grouped. As a commander divides his army into infantry, artillery, cavalry, air forces, quartermaster, engineer, and medical corps, so are the eternal forces divided into the seven purposes for the eternal conflict.

"The purposes of disintegration are more than seven. They divide into myriad motives as they fight the aspirations of immortal man. Free men choose freely how they will array themselves, but slaves are driven by their masters, visible or invisible, to fight for purposes not their own. Only when they have learned to discipline and develop their minds, as they now discipline and develop their bodies, may they choose freely the force with which they will be arrayed.

"Rich man against poor man. Capital against labor. State against offender. Poor man against wealth. Labor against development. Criminal against law. All are false distinctions.

"Seek ye the man of your own purpose, and cleave to him. If ye would build, seek a builder. If ye would heal, seek a healer. If justice absorb ye, seek a man furthering justice. But be not misled by the slave-driver, without or within. Beware of the bell-wether, and of personal or material motives. Govern yourselves first, and then choose ye whether to fight for progress or for disintegration, for unity or for destruction. Then choose ye the purpose ye will serve forcefully through eternity.

"This is the eighth lesson."

IX

"THIS is the ninth lesson.

"Men have lived in fear of forces from without, and have not perce ved that within themselves all forces are made potent. Men have feared purposes from without, and have not perceived that their own purpose is eternal. Men have talked of power, and failed to perceive its source. Men have dreamed of possession, and failed to find freedom. Possession is temporar and ephemeral. Freedom is ete nal. Should a man yield the freedom of his eternal purpose for any possession whatsoever?

"Build ye with all possessions, that purpose may be free For brotherhood commandeth service, and for this are possessions hallowed. He who hath, and denieth his brother opportunity, destroys his own purpose. He who hath possessions, and giveth his brother opportunity, builds for eternity. He who hath power and plenitude, and giveth his brother help, has given all men more than the one can take. He has built for eternity.

"The man who has this power to build with possessions for eternal progress has a force beside his own, the force of material purpose to aid his brother's force. Many there be who build for eternity with material possessions. They are the keepers of the keys for all who labor, stewards of opportunity.

"He who has opportunity to strive, and striveth not, destroys his own purpose. He who has the key to opportunity for building offered him, and fails to free the force, destroys both his own purpose and that of his brother.

"One purpose are all to serve—Progress. And whether it be with purpose and possessions, or with purpose and poverty, all serve equally who put their whole force into service.

"So may all men know they are brothers.

"This is the ninth lesson."

X

"THIS is the tenth lesson.

"The purposes of disintegration are these. Malice, Envy, Doubt, Falsehood, Ignorance, Lust, Cupidity, Fear. All these make for Destruction, which is the strong purpose that moves them all. Each of these is divided and subdivided into myriad motives of disintegration, many of which disguise themselves before daring to enter the consciousness of man.

"Malice and Envy present themselves most often as Light or Justice. Doubt as Light, Lust as Justice or Production, Cupidity as Building, Fear and Ignorance as Truth, and Destruction as Progress. But the disguises vary with the individual and with the moment, and the motives springing from these purposes are legion.

"Each individual in your life is a battle-ground of purposes that have fought from the moment the purposes of disintegration gathered one to another. Each man struggles to ally himself permanently with one or another of the purposes within him. Thus is it that a man whose desire is for light falls victim to malice, envy, and destruction; and he whose desire is production, to lust. Weakness of purpose is a subdivision of fear, and folly a minion of ignorance.

"All men aspire. Some with reluctance and halting, but all feel the purpose of progress working within them. They may mistake its nature or deny its power, but no man lives who has not felt its prompting. This is the purpose beyond all others, the Eternal Purpose of United Construction. No man can thwart it, no man can evade it, no force can defeat it. Why, then, oppose and delay it?

"Come, all ye who struggle and strive! Perceive once and forever the purpose of life, join now the forces of construction, and bring to all men Brotherhood.

"This is the tenth lesson."

XI

"THIS is the eleventh lesson.

"There is no man who has not force. He may be frail of body, weak of purpose, light of mind, faltering of step. Yet to some degree has he force, for without force personality cannot exist. There is no man so frail of body, so weak of purpose, so faltering of step, that he has not personality. There is no personality that is not a force for construction or for destruction. None that may not serve to build.

"There is no man so bound up in himself, so personal of motive, so narrow of vision, that he may not be turned from a deterrent force into a force for construction, save only those already given to purposes of disintegration.

"But no man is so vigorous of body, so firm of purpose, so profound of mind, so sure of step, that he may perfect his brother's life. 'Am I my brother's keeper?' has been transformed from a question uttered in defense of iniquity to an assertion uttered in defense of arrogance. 'Am I not my brother's keeper?'

"No man is his brother's keeper. The utmost that he may do for his brother is to arouse his brother's purpose, whether for construction or for destruction. Call to the purpose of Progress. Call to the seven purposes of construction. Help ye each brother to find the onward way. But if he will not answer, if calling fail to move him, then bid him destroy after his own purpose, that the fight may be open and his allegiance known of all men.

"Freedom to choose is the inalienable right of every human soul. Who hinders his brother's purpose delays the end of battle. Win him to progress, if he can be won by calling. Bid him declare himself, if he answer not the call. But he who coerces his brother, though it be toward construction, prolongs the struggle and delays the Great Purpose.

"No man is his brother's keeper.

"This is the eleventh lesson."

XII

"THIS is the twelfth lesson.

"Many men there be who fight for liberty and coerce their brothers.

"In war, all men must fight. But there is no man who may choose for another how his allegiance may be given.

"He who is not for progress is against it. He who has no allegiance that he will declare, is traitor to himself and to the purpose he follows. Cast him out and he will find his purpose known.

"So shall the opposing forces be clearly indicated. So shall each man find his own purpose clearly defined. So shall the wars within wars cease among men, and the fight be with you, as it is with us, between purposes and forces known and united, one against the other, until all purposes of destruction have been conquered and transformed, and the Great Purpose rendered free to progress to greater glories without end.

"This is the twelfth lesson."

NOTES

Asked to explain one phrase in the first Lesson, "the original purposes were all good," Mary K. said: "All were balanced. There is no evil that may not be good in proper combination. Evil is the gathered force of undirected and not fully animated good, combined in a destructive purpose by the attraction I mentioned."

An apparent contradiction of a statement in the first Lesson—"All pure purpose is fearless, whether for good or evil"—by one in the second Lesson—"The forces of disintegration are wily, but fearful. Bullies and cowards"—seemed to imply that forces of disintegration are not pure purpose. Mary K. explained: "They are pure purpose, fearless in pursuance of destruction, wily in bringing it about, brutal in consummating it, but cowards individually. Fearless of consequences when they pursue, but fearful when they fail. Like Germans."

Early in June, I discovered a relation between the definition of Eternal Purpose in the second paragraph of the third Lesson, and the divisions of the purpose of Progress near the end. "Eternal purpose is perfect justice (Justice), perfect fearlessness (Production), perfect understanding (Light), perfect honesty (Truth), perfect sympathy (Healing), perfect unity (Building), and eternal growth (Progress), which is progress perfectly expressed."

The end of the seventh Lesson seemed obscure, until the relation between its clauses was discovered. Written thus, its meaning is clear: "(1) No man is free who commands not himself. (2) No man is free who forgets his brother. (3) No man is free who fears to follow his purpose with all his force. (4) No man is free who fails to carry his share of the common load. He may have wealth and luxury, yet is he slave (1) *if he commands not himself.* He may be tempted by beauty (2) *to forget his brother,* yet is he slave, *if he commands not himself.* He may be frightened by calamity (3) *in following his purpose,* yet is he slave, *if he commands not himself.* He may be beaten by strangers (4) *while carrying his share of the common load,* yet is he slave *if he commands not himself."*

9th Lesson.

A curious inconsistency in the use of verbs will be noticed here, archaic and modern forms appearing in the same sentence repeatedly. This may have been due to my great fatigue when this lesson was taken, to the presence in the room of other persons, or to some condition or intention as yet unexplained.

10

Part III

" Science is the ladder by which life may quickly ascend, but until science recognizes a spiritual force as the one essential force, of which all other forces are incidental phenomena, progress must be limited."

" We have purpose to progress beyond the vision of man, but even material progress, to be constructive and permanent, must be governed by a vision beyond the day. We are trying to extend that vision."

I

IMMEDIATELY after the first Lesson had been given, Cass telephoned that the news from France was alarming. It was Saturday, March 23d. The great German offensive of 1918 had begun two days earlier, and the Allied forces were falling back, with appalling losses. I asked Mary K. whether she could tell us anything about it.

"Yes. It is a force of destruction, momentarily victorious, but Germany cannot win. She moves steadily toward her destruction."

Remembering our differing conceptions of time, I asked: "Do you speak in terms finite or infinite?"

"You will see her defeat soon, but the fight eternal will not be over with the end of the Great War. That will be only a temporary lull, and we shall have it all to do over and over, until conscious purpose ends it. *Do not fear.*" The emphasis is hers.

To be sure I had made no mistake, I pressed the inquiry again.

"You need not fear the end of the war. It is certain and inevitable. Germany is doomed, and must work her way back to light. This is not foreordained, but here we already see the end, and are looking toward the battles that will still be raging when the countries of the world seem peaceful."

[Some weeks later, this confident prophecy was slightly modified in its letter, though not in its spirit, when she said: "Unless the Allied purpose is undermined by forces of spiritual disintegration, Germany is doomed, but the fight must be kept up with confidence and consciously united force and purpose." This, however, merely emphasizes the teaching of all the lessons, that constructive purpose cannot find expression in passivity, that he who would live must fight, and that he who is not actively striving for progress is arrayed against it.]

As has been said, my knowledge of philosophies is of the slightest, and there is scarcely a suggestion contained in the first Lesson that was not new to me and entirely foreign to my habit of thought. Therefore, I sent a copy of it to Mr. Kendal, asking him to tell me whether the cosmic theory there outlined was familiar to him. Conscious of Mary K.'s summons, I took up a pencil.

"Tell Mr. Kendal the philosophers have perceived the truth in fragments. This is to be the whole truth, as far as it can be understood on your plane. It may sound, at moments, like a patchwork of philosophies, because all—or most—of them have some truth. He will help you in this. He found the truth in spite of philosophies, and it is part of his work to help others find it because of one—a philosophy not dreamed, but lived and proved and known. Therefore, not a philosophy, but a faith."

The next day, we dined with friends of that Anne Lowe for whom I had asked the first night Mary K. came to me, and from her long messages to them, a few may be quoted.

". . . It has always been easy for me to reach you, because you never doubted that I was there. Doubt is one of the things we cannot reach through. Doubt, bitterness, grief—all these are destructive forces." To a statement that they had felt deep grief, she returned: "You have not had the kind of grief that would shut me out. You have shut out some helpful forces, but you will do that no longer. It is because the force may reach you through me that I can come. We are the same purpose, and I can reach you freely. We can always reach those who are very near and dear. Sometimes people are dear to us there who are not really near us here. They do not need us, nor we them. It is an ephemeral relation. Love lasts eternally. Please don't ever forget that. . . . Listen to me. I cannot always reach you as directly as this, but just as soon as you learn to read my thoughts, as I now read yours, a messenger will not be necessary."

Briefly she explained to them the eternal significance of the Great War, the united purpose of Germany, and the failure of the Allies, thus far, to comprehend the essence of unity. Elizabeth, one of her friends, mentioned that it was like her to drop personalities for great issues, and she replied:

"The reason that I told you the thing I did about the great purposes and the eternal conflict is that I want you to realize a little of what it is all for, and to help you recognize the great ends toward which your problems lead. Build, build, never cease to build. Unite yourself to anybody who is of your purpose. Keep as clear as you can from entangling yourselves with forces of disintegration."

Miss S——, a teacher, and a stranger to me, was present, and after a little her brother took control of the pencil.

"You cannot realize how intimately we work

together still," was one of his assertions to her. "You are a fine force for progress. You are being and teaching the things we all work for here. Teach, above all, unity of purpose. Never mind the method. Look to the goal. Building, light, freedom, faith—these are what the forces of construction stand for, the way to the great purpose. The forces of disintegration are gathering for a tremendous fight. The Great War is one of the crises of civilization, but the battle to come still is one of the crises of eternity. It is for that we are preparing now. This is what we must say to all dear to us and, through them, to as wide a public as we can reach. . . . It is a great message that is to be given. To-day I only want you to be sure that I know all you feel and all you have suffered, and that the more confidently and freely you reach out to me, knowing I am there, the more easily and surely I can reach you."

Like the others, this man used the circle, which we were beginning to perceive must signify more than joy, as we understand the word. For example, on this occasion it was used thus: "You will look for me now, listen for me, feel me near you, and the (O) will be as near your life as it ever can be there." After telling her of the frequent use of this symbol, I asked him whether it had not a deeper significance—perhaps completion, perfection, consummate unity, something joyous of this larger sort, to which he replied in the affirmative.

A night or two after this, Cass suggested that we must make an effort to get into touch with David Bruce, but I said that we had asked about him several times, and that if he wished or needed to communicate with his family he would undoubtedly let me know. Aware of Mrs. Bruce's interest in psychic phenomena, I thought they might have established communication in some way. Within a few minutes I was conscious of a summons to the pencil.

First came Mary K.'s strong signature. Then, very quickly: "David Bruce is here, and wa . . ." There it ran off into nervous, illegible waves. When I said I could not follow, and asked that the message be more slowly given, it was resumed where it had been dropped. ". . . wants to talk to E . . . Bess." His wife's name is Elizabeth, and naturally was in my mind, but having written E, the pencil balked, delayed, crossed out the E, and finally wrote "Bess," firmly.

"Thank you," was the response to my promise to arrange the interview. For the first

time it occurred to me that possibly Mary K.
had given over the pencil, and I asked who
was writing, to be told quickly: "D. B."

Mrs. Bruce came the next day to talk to
him, and Mary K. told me, before her arrival,
to give her no details about the previous messages, adding: "He will tell her." And while
his opening message to her merely summarizes
similar assertions previously received, it is interesting as the first consecutive personal
statement of the survival of individuality in
the eternal pursuance of constructive purpose.

"I am here with you, darling Bess, as I
have been with you from the start," he began
at once. "You have known it all the time,
and I have been able to reach you in a way
that I can only describe to you as spiritual."

Here was the first veiled allusion, at first
rather puzzling, to that unknown force afterward mentioned by William James and others.

"We so long to tell you whom we love not
to grieve. We are of you, as you are of us.
Even more closely than we were when I was
visibly with you. Perfect union is only possible to pure spirit. That will come. Meanwhile, one of us is pure spirit, and both of us
so much the richer thereby. Once, in the beginning of things, you and I were the same

purpose. Purposes are eternal. They may be temporarily divided, temporarily overcome by the forces of disintegration, which are forever seeking to destroy, but forever each divided purpose answers to the call of its own. You and I were one purpose in the first, and we shall be perfectly reunited when you have joined me here. But while we were one in the beginning, one with many others of our great purpose, we are now eternally definite and separate individuals, but united as perfectly, after the first life there, as if we had returned to one unit. . . . The first message any of us send must be this one. That is the reason we can come so freely now and tell so much."

A little later, speaking of their children, he said: "All young people have battles to fight and problems to solve. Don't try to spare them that. It is thus they learn life's lessons, and the more they learn there the readier they will be to do the fine and glorious work here."

He had spoken before of being very busy, and now she commented: "He seems so interested in the work!"

"Interested is not the word. It's more like inspiration."

"Was the passing difficult?" she asked.

"Not difficult at all. The pain ended with unconsciousness."

"But you had no pain!"

"Yes, I had some—not expressed, nor quite definite. Difficult to explain until experienced. Words do not convey the sensation. Not quite fear, not quite pain, but a strange moment of suffering. Then consciousness again, beauty, force, perfectly clear perceptions, but a period of something approaching incredulity." I mentioned Frederick's statement that he had been "dazed by the bigness of it," and Mr. Bruce went on. "That's it. The bigness of it is indescribable, and so extraordinarily lovely and high that it is not readily realized or grasped."

She said she had dreaded to have him go alone, and asked whether some one met him.

"Yes, we are very tenderly received. There is always a part of one's own purpose waiting."

"Have you seen Jack?"

"Yes; he is still a little bewildered, but will soon be in fighting trim again." This young man had been killed in an accident.

"'In fighting trim'!" she repeated. "How funny!"

"No, it isn't funny. We fight perpetually, and love it. It is a wonderful thing to fight with the great forces, and to know why. Most of those in your life fight in confusion and doubt, and suffer. But here we unite ourselves to a definite and constructive purpose, and the fight is glorious."

"Do you see Granny?"

"No. She has gone on to a life beyond ours. She will come back, some day, and I will see her."

"You have helped me very much by believing that I lived," he told her, at another point. "It is very hard for us to be put aside. . . . We know here how intimately our life and yours are lived together, and the one almost intolerable thing is to have our dear ones live and believe that we do not. It defers things so. . . . It hurts us when the apparent separation is made real."

"I hope you won't get so far beyond that I can't catch up," she said.

"Never! You will begin farther along than I did. We shall go on together now, for eternity. Since you know that I am with you, and especially as we live and work consciously together, we shall grow together."

"Did I do all I could for you, at the last? Did you feel my fear?"

"No, I did not feel your fear. But when one knows that the step is coming, there is one blinding moment of dread. . . . You kept me a little while," he continued, when she said that she had tried to hold him here, "but the thing had gone too far."

"Was there anything we could have done that was not done?"

"Nothing. It had to be." But when she inferred that the time had come for him to take up work in the next plane, he protested. "No. Nothing like that is 'intended.' There is no foreordination. It is all a matter of forces, constructive and destructive. My material energy was too little to withstand the material forces of destruction. My flesh yielded. That has no real relation to eternal force. . . . One serves one's purpose, here or there. I am doing better work here than I could have done there, but that has no relation or part in death. It is entirely a physical thing."

"Did —— make you nervous?"

"No mere man could make me fail to respond to your call to courage. I knew and you knew, that it might be the end of life there; but there was no possible thing that you could have done, mentally, physically, or spiritually, that you did not do. It was your courage that kept me calm, even through that dread moment; your spirit that met me when I woke here; your tenderness that soothed my first bewilderment; your purpose that roused me to better, broader, finer work than I had ever dreamed before. It has been you —you and I, one always—that have helped and upheld me, as your faith has enabled me to reach and uphold you."

This interview took place in the afternoon, and with a good deal of incidental conversation, covered several hours, leaving me very tired. But after dinner the familiar summons warned me that my services were again in demand. I took up a pencil, and Mary K. announced the second Lesson, which followed rapidly, with the same unhesitating flow that had characterized the first one.

II

MEANWHILE, happy letters were coming almost daily from the Gaylord family, and less frequently, but with expressions of equal conviction, from Mr. Kendal.

Mrs. Gaylord had promised to spend Easter week with relatives, in a Middle Western town, which she had not visited—indeed, had scarcely dared to think of—since taking Frederick's body there for burial; and the day after the second Lesson was given she arrived in New York, where she paused briefly *en route*, her elder daughter and son-in-law joining her the next morning.

Although her train arrived late in the evening, we talked a little to Frederick before separating for the night. We had been commenting on her changed appearance.

"Mother dearest, you are not much differenter than I am," he began, after the usual signature.

"Why, Frederick!" she exclaimed. "Are you better, too?"

149

He made the enthusiastic little circle so often used. "(O) So much better! You can't guess how much better I am. It helps me as much as it does you."

"Were you at Mrs. Z——'s the other day?" she asked, referring to a visit to a "medium," of which I had not been informed.

"I was that, but she fell down on what I was trying to get over," was the reply. When his mother said she had not received what she expected on that occasion, he returned: "Nor what we expected. . . . She's all right, as far as she goes." He told her, also, that the woman accompanying him, described by Mrs. Z——, had been his father's mother.

"This is a nice, peaceful powwow we're having to-night," he commented, when they had exchanged views concerning various personal matters. "I had to work last time, but this time I'm here for . . ."

The pencil paused, and I asked: "For what?"

"Just for a good time, Mrs. L——. Sis is coming to the party to-morrow. Hooray!"

A little later, when she expressed some uncertainty about her ability to go through an Easter in K——, with all its sad associations, unshaken, he warned her: "Don't you go backsliding!" Continuing, she told us that his last illness had developed just before Easter, and that in his desire to give the family an unclouded day he had persuaded a friend to send them a typewritten letter, which he signed, containing no intimation of his illness.

"I'll write you a letter this Easter with a lot more pep in it," he promised. "You go on and have your Easter presents, and flowers, and eggs, and all, and when you begin backsliding, stop . . . look . . . listen [1] . . . and I'll be on the crossing, ringing the bell."

With an ejaculation of surprise, his mother told us that she had been recently in the home of a traffic expert, whose large hall was strikingly decorated with signs for the regulation of traffic.

"I believe that's what he's thinking of!" she exclaimed.

"Sure, you've got it! I'll ask Sis to buy you a bell for me, to remind you."

This diversion had completely banished the gathering sadness of her reminiscences, and she began talking of Washington, whence she had come, saying that there seemed to be a good deal of pessimism in official circles concerning war conditions. It will be remembered that the bombardment of Paris, by a long-distance gun, began March 23d.

[1] Each of these words was written in larger script than the preceding one.

"There are lots of things Washington doesn't know," Frederick assured her. "The end of the war must come soon."

We wondered, as I had before, how much difference there was between his conception of time, as indicated by the word "soon," and ours.

"None of us can name the day and hour, but we see the inevitable end coming soon. Germany knows she is weakened, but doesn't know why. We do, and we have told you. No nation on earth can fight this fight alone, deserted by all purposes, both for good and evil, and with only one force left—Fear."

[Long afterward, Mary K. said to me, in this connection: "We see the awakening purpose of forces for progress in your life, and are able to help them in proportion to the vigor with which that purpose is put into action. Germany, on the other hand, fights now with only physical power. Eternal forces are implacably against her, and the forces of destruction have abandoned her. She has no ally here now. Her unity is destroyed, while ours is strengthening. The only danger, as far as the war is concerned, lies in a weakening of actual purpose, forcefully expressed in action. We are your allies, answering your call and inciting you to endeavor. When Germany began this war she had superhuman strength, which the world was unprepared to meet, but for every vibration of pure constructive purpose among the Allied forces we have added two, and only a weakening of your purpose can defeat us now. Every individual among you who fails to strive for victory with all his strength invites disaster."]

Frederick's talk with his mother was brief that night, and when she arose, to return to her hotel, he said: "Good night. I am going home with you, if I may."

This seemed to Cass and me a curious phrase, under the circumstances, and we also commented upon his generous use of slang, especially in the latest interview, wondering whether it were characteristic of him.

The next morning his sister, Mrs. Wylie, arrived with her husband, to spend a day with Mrs. Gaylord in New York. It chanced that they had been away from home for several weeks and had seen none of Frederick's manuscript, nor any copy of it. As she read—from the original roll—his messages of the preceding evening, she constantly exclaimed: "How characteristic!" and his closing phrase brought tears to her eyes. She told me, then, that along with a copious use of slang, Frederick had preserved an odd little formality of phrase, even in his closest personal relations—a trait not common to other members of the family.

Later, in glancing for the first time through the typewritten record of earlier interviews, again and again she expressed astonishment at the characteristic quality of his phraseology, which had not been mentioned to me before. Mrs. Gaylord had spoken of her vivid consciousness of his personality, imbuing all he said to her, and had told me, during the earlier days of this intercourse, more or less about his habit of thought, but it is characteristic of her to ignore minor details, and only when Mrs. Wylie arrived did I learn anything about his habit of speech.

"Frederick," he announced, when we invited communication, his bold signature stretching across the whole width of the paper. "Hello, Sis! This is too good not to be true! Hello, Dick!" This to Mr. Wylie, whose marriage to his sister had taken place during the last weeks of his illness. "Welcome home to the family! We're all in it now, for good and all. This is the thing we've all needed, I almost as much as the rest of you, but I did know that sooner or later it must come, so I could bear it better than you could."

It must not be understood that all these communications came as consecutively as they are presented here. There were frequent pauses; sometimes because of our preoccupation in conversation; sometimes, apparently, because of difficulties of transmission not explained. Occasionally I stopped to verify a word or a phrase, asking if it had been correctly taken, and with increasing frequency the pencil returned without suggestion from me, to cross out false starts. Some of the latter, which seemed significant, will be indicated from time to time. The following message, however, came rapidly, without pause.

"We are all of kindred purposes. That's the reason we cling to each other so. Family hasn't a thing to do with it. It was our good fortune to have no forces of disintegration in our immediate group. We are all builders, in one way or another. Not all in the same way, but all for the great purpose. This is one of the things I have wanted to say to you. Don't be misled by transient relationships of that life. Respect them, but don't be eternally influenced by them, because when you get over here you'll find that some of the people you've thought you were most fond of have simply dropped out. You don't need them, nor they you. Find your purposes clearly, and stick to them. We all have purpose, but not all of you there have found out just what yours is.

Find it, and follow it fearlessly. There, that's off my chest!"

Mr. Wylie spoke of the "upside-down stunt," of which some one had written him, and I said it had been done chiefly to convince me—to show me, in Frederick's phrase, "who was running it."

"You know now who is running it," he contributed, "but you're certainly formal with strangers!"

In the midst of some talk of ours, the pencil swung off with vigor, writing, "Sis!" in huge script, like a joyous exclamation, ending in strong circles. "Just wait till I catch Dad!" he went on. "And Babe, too! All of us together! Margaret will have to forget her formality then, I tell you!"

Mrs. Wylie mentioned the common impression that personality must be transmuted by death into something remote and strange— that only the soul survived. "Of course, we love the soul of any one dear to us," she said. "But, after all, the thing we know best, and therefore love best, is the habit of thought— the characteristic mental attitude, and it is so wonderful to find Frederick unchanged— just like himself."

"Sure! Why not?" he returned. "You people must learn that this isn't 'like himself.' It *is* himself. Right here on the job."

"Those words!" His mother and sister exchanged startled glances. Then they told me that just before his long struggle for life on this plane ended, when during six months his powers of recuperation had repeatedly astonished surgeons and nurses, he opened his eyes, to find his father bending over him, and whispered for the last time: "On the job."

"I've always been on it since, too," he rapidly assured them, "and longing to tell you so. You never can know, until you try it, how we hate to be left out. We're on the job as you can't even imagine, and it makes us sort o' sick that we can't get it over to you of our own love and purpose."

He interrupted the talk following this with: "Trot along to lunch! I want to start going and not stop. Get it over, do!"

So we trotted, and got it over as soon as possible, though throughout the meal he insisted upon having a voice in the conversation, writing messages on all the blank paper we had about us, and over the backs of the available menu cards.

"You can't lose me, and needn't try," he told me, and when I protested that he was making it impossible for me to finish my luncheon, he retorted: "You have a perfectly good left hand. Eat with that."

Several times Mr. Wylie expressed his interest in what he called "the upside-down stunt," and when we were again seated about a writing-table, Frederick "demonstrated."

"Incidentally, Dick," he mentioned, starting at my right and writing toward my left, "you wanted to see this work. Well, here you are. This is the way it is done."

As this began, Mrs. Gaylord smiled, pulling her chair nearer to the table, where she could watch every movement of the pencil.

"Sit up closer, Mother dearest," Frederick continued, "and everybody hold hands." Looking slightly bewildered, she held out her hands to the others. I said that he had used a figure of speech, but she thought he had meant it literally, and we referred the question to him. "Yes, all but your writing-hand," he said; so we all joined hands, and I asked why.

"Just to make us know more surely that we are all one and indivisible, from now on through eternity. Easter resurrection for every one of us. We are all born again, to some extent, by our communion in this way; I more than you, because I have left the flesh behind. But to you has come new life, new force, new purpose, new faith, through your touch with this life of pure spirit. It is truly your resur-

rection. This is your Easter message. Hail!
And be happy ever after!"

I anticipated none of this message, and its
tenor surprised me greatly. Before I had re-
covered from my astonishment Mrs. Gaylord
exclaimed: "That must be the Easter letter
he promised me!" Immediately he signed it.
"Frederick, to Mother and all of you."

We spoke of the relation of this whole
revelation to orthodox religion, and some one
said that it was not in accordance with the
Bible.

"Yes, it is," he contradicted. "You have
never learned to read the Bible in this light.
The great prophecies have always been phrased
in the language, and more or less in the spirit,
of the time in which they were uttered. This
is the first time in the history of the world
when physical science has been sufficiently
advanced to enable us to tell the people the
truth in terms they would truly understand.
Prophecies have been veiled, apparently, not
because the truth was vague, but because men
were not prepared to understand it in all its
details. Nor are they now. But this is to be
the whole truth, as far as it can be understood
now by your prophets and people. And for
the first time it is possible to give it to you
directly in this way, without pretense or mys-

tery, book or bell, a natural law operating naturally and freely, through an accredited messenger who makes no claim to inspiration."

In the course of our drifting talk his mother remembered that Mrs. Z—— had tried to convey a warning through her from Frederick to Mr. Wylie, but had been unable to tell her what it concerned. After some effort to discover its connection, suggesting possible journeys or business ventures, Mrs. Z—— had finally said that Dick was about to do something, she did not know what; but whatever it was, Frederick said he must not do it. Mrs. Gaylord now asked Frederick what he had intended to say.

"She didn't get my message. I was trying to tell him not to be fearful about anything." Mr. Wylie is sometimes prey to nervous apprehension and worry. "It keeps us back and we can't help him as we're trying to do. Open up, Dick! Let us in and we'll all pull together." This apparently touched some situation unknown to me, for Mr. and Mrs. Wylie exchanged glances, and instantly Frederick made his quick circles. "(O) That's it! Now we're off! No, it isn't incredible," he added, replying to some comment of theirs. "It's the truest thing you ever heard. But Mrs. Z—— can't get beyond externals."

This seems to be a very good example of the way certain messages are confused by the persons through whom they come. In this case, while the intended warning was conveyed, a purely subjective and spiritual message was so distorted, however unconsciously and unintentionally, that it was given an objective and material significance.

Asked whether an acquaintance of theirs would be helped by a knowledge of their intercourse with him, he said: "She is not ready for this yet. Few people, comparatively, are free enough to accept it. It has been forbidden by the church, ridiculed by the laity, and labelled 'poison, don't touch' by neurologists and the scientific, half-baked intellectuals."

"Fake mediums have done a lot to bring it into disrepute," Mr. Wylie suggested.

"That's the reason for some of it. Another reason, less obvious to you, but equally potent, is that people who had the sensitiveness to be messengers frequently lacked the purpose of truth fundamentally, and though thinking they were honest, entertained devils unaware. . . . That is the reason so many people have gone to pieces, mentally and physically. The purposes of disintegration caught them and destroyed them. But this time, we beat them to it."

"All philosophies have had some foundation of truth," he told us, a little later, "or they would not have been permitted to live. This new faith will be attacked by the disintegrating forces, in an attempt to discredit it as a patchwork of philosophies. The new truths they will ignore, or flatly deny. But this is the whole truth, as far as it can be told now. Believe it, follow it, preach it, live it, and we shall truly build that structure I told you of, Mother dearest, of force, light, and sweetness —which is you. I seem to be doing a darned lot of preaching!"

"It isn't like you, either," his mother remarked.

"You see, we've got to get this over. It's imperative."

At that, she said it was like him, after all, because he had always talked eagerly to the family about his "job," whatever it might be, adding: "Is it 'imperative' because of the war and the sorrow? Or because the time is ripe?"

"It's because there's the very devil of a fight coming, and we've got to gather every force we have, and unite it."

"Is beating the Germans helping the constructive force? Or is the war merely the awakening through suffering?"

"Germany has been united in purpose as a

destructive force for many years. They gave themselves deliberately, not as individuals, but as a people, to what parsons call the powers of darkness. We know them to be forces of disintegration, which found in Germany their strongest ally in the civilized world. We've been fighting Germany and her purposes here for years, I find. Suffering makes people readier to listen to truth, but beating Germany was as necessary to the world's health as sanitation to a hospital."

"That's a clear and explicit statement," some one said.

"We are perfectly definite and explicit about questions of eternal purpose. The difficulty with most people is that they want to know how much U. S. Steel will go up next Tuesday, or whether to give the baby soothing-syrup."

After some interchange concerning his father and younger sister, he said, "I want to write them an Easter greeting." So we got a fresh roll of paper, and he wrote a brief but tender letter, which was sent to them that night.

"Which one of us will be best able to do this?" Mrs. Wylie asked.

". . . The time will come when this sort of thing is unnecessary. We can talk without material aid. . . . We never know when the power is going to develop. It's much like an electric current. You never know it's there until you feel it—until your signal comes over the wire..... Try it out, all of you. We know no more about who can do it than you do, except in cases of extraordinary power." Some time afterward, however, he warned them of the dangers of attempting to handle this force, intimating that great conservation of energy in other directions should accompany the endeavor.

His mother spoke of his being happy, and he returned: "Perfectly happy now, thank you. It's the eternal thing, really started. I hate to have this party break up, but anyhow it isn't for long. I've been away longer, when I lived there, than I shall be now, and we are all of us as sure of the next meeting, and the next good time, as we were then."

"He knows it is ending, and we must go to our trains," Mrs. Gaylord said.

"Not ending at all. Beginning! *Hooray!*"

On that triumphant note they took their departure, Mrs. Gaylord westward bound, the Wylies to New England; but, owing to a defective timepiece, both missed their trains. Within an hour, Mrs. Wylie telephoned me that her mother had caught—by the narrowest margin—a later train, hoping to secure sleeping-accommodation after leaving, a dubious venture in these days of diminished service and crowded trains. We arranged to dine and spend the evening together.

Afterward, it occurred to me that Frederick might prefer to be with his mother that night, and I asked Mary K. about it.

"Frederick has engaged his mother in (O) . . ."

"What does that mean now?" I interrupted. "Bliss?"

"Yes . . . and will come here to-night to see the others."

12

III

Like the rest of the family, Mrs. Wylie feared the effect of the Western visit upon her mother's new-found tranquillity of spirit, and she was also uneasy lest Mrs. Gaylord had been unable to secure Pullman accommodations.

"Mother is all right and happy," Frederick told us, in the evening. "She is still reading her precious book"—a copy of his earlier interviews, which she carried with her.

Some one asked whether he meant that her general condition was "all right," or that she was "all right" on the train.

"On the train. She's blissful!"

This was verified a day or two later by a letter from Mrs. Gaylord, in which she said: "I came away filled with strength and calm and joy." She also mentioned casually that she had found a vacant section on the train, and traveled comfortably.

"How does purpose combat forces of evil?" Mr. Wylie asked.

"It is done by overpowering them, as the sun dispels mist, separating them into smaller particles or units. And when that is impossible, by driving them like clouds before a high wind. They work for evil, but can be separated sometimes from the mass and united with constructive forces. Only small fragments of the main forces can be so converted, at present. Mostly we rout them."

"Does an evil soul lose personality?" his sister questioned. "Is it absorbed, or broken into fragments?"

"The individuality that finds its first expression in your life is never absorbed or broken up. I speak of the forces of disintegration, composed of more individuals than the greatest army, as being routed. We mass ourselves and our purposes against them and theirs, when we fight in the open here. But as has been explained in the Lessons, the very material form you have was originally an effort to evolve a force not conquerable by purpose alone. Both good and evil forces, in your phrase—constructive and destructive, in ours—took possession of these concrete forms, and now the bitterness of the fight is greatest where both forces are represented in one individual. The only way we can fight that effectively is to sit on the job, and try to call to the purpose that is ours more clearly and appealingly, or more commandingly, than the other fellow does. That's the reason we are begging you now to work with us. A great crisis is at hand, and we want you to meet it consciously in your life there, knowing its nature, so that we can have your help, not only in withstanding material onslaughts, like Germany's invasions and brutality, but in things of the spirit—the real things, the eternal things—so that together we may win a real victory. The individual whose purposes are fundamentally destructive is not damned nor lost. He is just delayed. Sooner or later he must work his way up, and it is entirely up to him whether he does it sooner or later—after he reaches this life, especially. In your life, he is sometimes confused or misled. He pays for that, too—not pays, but makes good for it, by working here for the development he had not sense enough to take there. But his delay is brief, beside that of the essentially destructive force."

A little later, Mrs. Wylie spoke again of her uneasiness about her mother's visit to K——, and some one suggested telegraphing her that Frederick had been with us that evening.

"Give her my love when you wire," he directed, "and tell her I'm on the crossing, still ringing that bell. Don't you worry, Sis. I'll go and stay with her most of the time she's there, and she'll know it. I'll come to you, Easter, too, for a little while. . . . Tell Dad I'll be taking care of Mother. He needn't fret about it."

"Do you want me to look up 'Bob' and tell him about his little girl?" she asked.

He replied, "Yes, do." And when she asked if he could give her something more definite than a Christian name by which to trace this unknown man among his large and scattered acquaintance, he wrote the name of a Middle Western city, adding: "You can find out from the fellows. All of them know Bob."

This seems to be a case of marked deflection of ray, to use Mr. Kendal's simile, for up to the day when this manuscript goes to the printer the Gaylord family have been unable to identify "Bob," although there was a confused intimation, late in April, that Mrs. Z——— had made a mistake in the name, and a suggestion that the surname was Roberts. It is not impossible that this was one of those wily incursions of disintegrating force, with intent to confuse, to which we afterward grew accustomed.

On Friday and Saturday of that week (March 29th and 30th), there were interviews of great interest, but of too personal a character to be extensively quoted.

Replying to the inquiry of a man for his father, Mary K. said: "He was a great force here, but has passed on into the life beyond ours. He can and will return to talk to you, but not immediately."

"Tell G—— the constructive forces are working for him, as he for them," was the answer to questions about a man in this life. "Temporary disappointments are unimportant. Do not fear. We build together, and surely. The result is certain and for his purpose—progress, light, and justice. His individual concern is to have faith, follow his purpose, and trust us. The only failure possible comes from admitting doubt, disintegration, and fear."

An expression of anxiety concerning another man on this plane was met thus: "N—— has felt his own purpose stirring a little. . . . A perfectly good purpose when he finds it. He has had many forces fighting, within and without. He will wake when this message is given to the world. He is too intelligent not to recognize truth as obvious as this will be." Some one asked when this would occur. "When Margaret completes the book she will publish soon." This was the first intimation of the way in which I was expected to carry out Mary K.'s instructions to make this experience known, concerning which we had wondered not a little.

It was suggested that a member of this person's family might help him, from the next plane, but this was said to be impossible, as they were not of the same purpose.

"The family connection is nothing here. His own purposes know him, both good and bad, and they are fighting it out. He has answered first one, then another. But fundamentally he is for justice. He will answer to that in the end. . . . Sometimes he will shut it all out and yield to the forces seeking to destroy him, but he will fight in the end for freedom and justice."

"She is not of our forces," was the reply to an inquiry about an artist who left this life twenty years ago. This was crossed out, however, and "not mentally free" substituted.

When I was alone, I asked Mary K. about this woman, and she returned: "She is not a destructive force, but is deterrent. She is working out problems not met when she should have met them, and is fighting for growth, just as she soon or late will fight for progress.

She fights for herself, her own growth, and not for progress in the larger sense."

Afterward, I learned, from some one who knew her well, of this woman's devouring and unquenchable ambition for supremacy in her profession.

Whimsical Anne Lowe, writing to three friends of her continued association with them, said: "Believe—*know*—that we are a positive force, and united we stand, hurrah! Our faith helps all beneficent purpose. Its force is freed and multiplied by the sum of your participation."

"I wonder if she could tell us what our purposes are?" Elizabeth said.

"Yours is Progress, Ruth's is Light, Katharine's is Healing and Light. You are blended. Elizabeth to push, Ruth to illumine and interpret, Katharine to understand and soothe."

Ruth said, wistfully: "Then all I can do is to shine?"

"Interpreters are really prophets," she was told. "That is all the greatest prophets ever were. You are of their purpose, so cheer up!"

Interrupting a little discussion as to whether dominant purpose is born in us or developed, she said: "We are born with many purposes, latent and striving, but as we live we make daily choice."

That evening, our old friend Maynard Holt came for a long talk. After some entirely personal exchange, Cass spoke of Maynard as having been, in this life, a believer in individualism.

Beginning with some allusion to former discussions between them, concerning what he called "the temporary manifestations of Socialism," Maynard replied: "Now I can tell you definitely that the salvation of the civilized world is dependent on the independence of the individual. . . . It's a big and glorious period in eternal history. The time has almost come for the open fight. Prepare your ground carefully, and gird up your loins for combat. It's coming."

A little later, in a similar connection, he said: "The conscious co-operation of purpose is the only sound principle of Socialism. That is eternally sound. And now that we are consciously and forcefully working in harmony with the great and eternal purpose, they can't stop us."

"Has this new opportunity of communication with this plane made you over there happier?" he was asked.

"It has opened an entirely new channel to us here in this part of the world. In the Far East, we have the channel, but no hard-pan to support the stream. Here science gives us a foundation from which to work, but we have had no channel through which to reach it.... Everywhere in the civilized world the minds of intelligent people have turned to this. There is reaching and questioning and longing, and a dawning faith."

At this time I did not know how frequently belief in the possibility of communication with those in a life beyond is accompanied by an inclination toward the Oriental philosophies, but Maynard's allusion to the Far East was given greater significance by the replies to later questions.

To an inquiry concerning the possible influence of these teachings in Germany, he returned: "They are a philosophical and abstract-minded people, and they'll be hunting a plausible and satisfactory explanation of themselves before long. And this is less uncomplimentary than the others will be, besides having the undeniable advantage of being true, which they will have learned, by that time, to appreciate."

"Can't those with eyes, ears, and understanding learn wisely to control, lead, and uplift the mass?" Cass asked. "In Russia, for example?"

"Don't be in such a hurry. There's all

eternity, and evolution is slow. But the mills of the gods grind on, and the grist is sure. The Russians, like the Germans, must climb their own hills. America has a few to climb, too. This will help many, uplift a few, escape the mass, but leaven the whole. There is no millennium at hand. This is just a light by which the path is made more clear. It will influence many thousands, in many countries, but the inert mass must work its way on, through the old channels of evolution, made easier by knowledge and by experience of those ahead, but not to be evaded or avoided by any miracle."

"But it will bring conscious purpose and effort to bear in helping this evolution?"

"Surely. It is a message eagerly awaited and desired."

Later that evening, I asked Mary K. whether she could tell me anything about the book Anne Lowe had said I was to publish.

"Yes. It must be ready for publication by Fall."

"Evidently sordid, material details of book manufacture escape your attention," I said, laughing. "This is the thirtieth of March, and you have not yet given me all the material for your book. When you have done that, it still must be edited, assembled for publication, copied, accepted by publishers, printed, and sold. Perhaps you don't know that salesmen for publishing-houses begin taking orders for Fall publications in June, and generally carry sample copies of the books with them?"

She said I would have the necessary material in a month or six weeks, and that editing would "take another month," from which it is evident that no eight-hour law is operative on her plane. She also advised me to see publishers at once, tell them what was happening, read them parts of communications already received, and arrange for Fall publication, conditional upon their satisfaction with the completed manuscript—which, not without misgivings concerning such procedure, I immediately prepared to act upon.

A night or so later, Maynard Holt came again, with his mother, who said: "Maynard brought me to call."

When we asked if she worked with those on this plane, she replied: "Yes, but also with undeveloped purposes, here before their time."

Returning to the subject of Russian upheaval, Maynard said: "They are goners for some time, now. It will take them long to assemble their purposes again constructively."

"If you had been here," Cass asked, "would

you have viewed the Russian situation and its effect on the world as you do now?"

"Not quite, I think. We see farther ahead, and have sounder premises from which to argue than you've ever had there."

"This plan, of course, includes all the people of the world," Cass continued. "Are those who leave here undeveloped, still undeveloped there?"

"There is a large and growing population here of the undeveloped," was Maynard's reply, "which is one of the lesser reasons for our keen desire to purposize the world."

IV

"WHAT place have the unfit on your plane?"
we asked Mary K., at the conclusion of the
sixth Lesson.

"No place. They are errors of development, and have a long struggle ahead before
they can reach the degree of development that
should have been theirs in your life. They
are fusions of weak purposes, and should not
be permitted to hold back the strong and the
fit. Development will come to them slowly,
at best, but more quickly here than there."

"In the present stage of our development,
is there a sufficient incentive to progress, without hope of material gain or personal improvement?"

"Any material gain that is for the constructive purpose is a force for light and progress
in the larger sense. Material gain is deterrent
only when purpose is its price. Personal ambition is an incentive always. When it is for
personal gain, at any price, it is deterrent.
When it is ambition to serve a great purpose

worthily, it becomes a constructive force, to which material gain adds only more constructive force."

"Have you all history spread out before you? Or are you taught after you get there?"

"We have a grasp of results, not easily understood in your life. It is like seeing a landscape from a high and distant hill. The salient features are easily distinguished."

"Are these messages for all people? Or only for civilized people? Do they come from Christians on your plane?"

"This is a message to the civilized world. . . . Jew or Gentile, Christian or agnostic, all men are brothers in the larger sense. Uncivilized little brothers will grow, or come to this freer plane to join their larger purposes."

"Then from whom do these Lessons come?"

"From great constructive purposes. There is no sect or creed, color or prejudice, here."

Saturday, April 6th, Mrs. Bruce came again to talk to her husband, and he thanked her for a public gift which she had just made in his name, promising such co-operation in the work it promoted as could be given from his plane. She said that she had felt suddenly impelled to make this contribution, and had acted at once upon the impulse.

"You all feel impelled to work with us as

soon as you realize we are here near you," he told her, "and the things we can do together are as yet undreamed in your life."

She spoke of his former interest in the arts, . which he said he had left behind as "material manifestations." Discussing the relation of artistic expression to constructive purpose, he said: "Art, when it is a real interpretation of life, is a high and noble thing, but the art that is merely self-expression is a disintegrating force. Too much of it is that now."

At that time, she had read none of the Lessons, and he told her of the seven purposes of construction, continuing: "To purpose of any nature only similar purpose calls, and when the call is heard there is no choice but to answer. No choice after the call has been admitted to consciousness. It may be shut out and denied, but once listened to, whether for construction or for destruction, the answer is bound to come. That is why we so insistently urge the discovery of purpose and the beauty of construction. Character, as you understand it, results from the purposes admitted to consciousness. Not always recognized, but always let in."

He had some difficulty in getting one word written, and she spoke of his erasures of wrong starts as extraordinary and unusual.

"Not a bit unusual, if you think how often the words of your languages fail as convincing and accurate symbols. You often correct them yourselves. A translation may be made in any of several ways, depending on the reactions of the translator to certain symbols. So, when Margaret reacts freely, we let it stand. When she fails, wholly or in part, we correct it."

In view of later statements concerning the force used in these manifestations, I assume this to mean, not that I make the translation mentioned, but that certain symbols used in translation are sometimes difficult to convey through me. Frequently other words have been substituted for those originally begun, when there was trouble in writing them. Another explanation of these occasional difficulties of transmission was suggested afterward, first by Frederick and later more explicitly by Mary Kendal.

"Do you see us visibly?" Mrs. Bruce asked.

"Yes, of course. We see all you do, and more. We see motives, where you see appearance."

[Long afterward (May 26th), Mr. Kendal asked Anne Lowe whether she could see sunsets, and she replied: "No, but we see their equivalent in dawn of purpose."

[She had previously expressed approval of a

room, which had been arranged with great
care for one dear to her, and he asked whether
she saw its physical details, or only its effects
upon the minds of persons entering it, to which
her answer was: "We never see material
things. We see their significance."

[Similarly, Mary K. said (May 31st), "We
read your thought frequently, and always perceive motive, intention, and the mental and
spiritual significance of your reactions to material things, in themselves unimportant. So
we say we see the thing itself, because we perceive its essential significance."]

Mrs. Bruce said her daughter wanted to
know whether dogs continue to exist after life
here, feeling that they must.

"They do not come as animals, exactly.
But there is no manifestation of force that is
not purpose, and purposes are united and
gather here, in ways not possible for you to
understand, in the progress toward the great
purpose." Ten days later, Frederick stated
this more explicitly.

After a pause, Mr. Bruce said: "We are so
full of our fine but tremendous task here, at
this great moment of crisis, that I'm afraid
I'm not very entertaining. We talk shop to
you, because that is the reason we can come
so freely now."

"You refer to the great crisis?" she asked. "Not to our present crisis here?"

"Germany is bereft of all purpose. Purposes of destruction have left her. She has one sole, frantic force remaining—fear. After that, destruction, long followed, will turn and rend her, and fear will be lost in despair."

"Aren't there some good Germans?" she suggested, adding that their daughter thought it unfair to condemn a whole people for the sins of some of them.

"Many good Germans have admitted to consciousness the call of destructive purposes, and have for the moment joined forces against us. For many years this preparation has been going on. No German who has ever admitted the forces of disintegration is quite free from them now. There were some officers who took their own lives and faced the consequences, rather than join forces with the dominant purpose of their people. No person can live in Germany now who is not party to disintegration. No German lives in the world, who still calls himself German, who is not party to disintegration."

"You say they have 'joined forces against us for the moment,'" I mentioned.

"Some of them will see light, and build forcefully for true progress. Some of them will destroy while they live. Some will be for years deterrent, and the end is impossible to foresee."

A day or two after this, when I was alone, I asked Mary K. what Mr. Bruce meant by saying that once the call of purpose is admitted to consciousness, there is no choice but to answer.

"He meant that your personal struggle is only with the purposes admitted to consciousness. All forces are constantly trying to reach you, to enlist you for the great struggle. Once admitted to your consciousness, you have no choice but to answer, and the struggle between opposing forces is fought with your help. Many waver between the two, now lending aid to this one, now to that. A few choose instantly; some to progress, some to delay, some to build, some to destroy. This is what men call character."

"He said also that no German who has ever admitted to consciousness the forces of disintegration is quite free from them now. Why?"

"Because there is in your life, as here, a group loyalty. But whereas here we are grouped by purpose, there you are grouped largely by geographical location. And any German who justified this war in the beginning is party to disintegration to some extent still. His group loyalty holds him, though his purpose protest. That will be the final test. Purpose, or finite loyalty to finite group."

One or two interesting statements were made, about this time, during an interview with the widow of a well-known New York surgeon.

"Your husband's work is healing still," Mary K. told her. After enumerating the constructive purposes, she continued: "Healing was always his purpose, and he follows it still, with all his great force. He has a freer field here, and fulfils his purpose fully. That is the reason he is unable to be here to-day. The Germans are liberating many bewildered and fear-stricken souls, and all our great healers are held by their need."

When we spoke of ways of finding happiness she said: "Who fears the purpose he should serve with force destroys it. Fear not. Find it, serve it, and happiness of a positive kind will find you. . . . Your force is scattered among many latent purposes. Find the dominant call of Progress to your soul, and follow that, leaving the rest behind."

Again, a day or two later, the present preoccupation of healers on the next plane was mentioned, when I asked Mary K. whether a certain woman would come at a given time to meet friends who had asked for her.

"She may. I shall try to have her here," she said. "Her work is healing, and all our healers are working constantly. . . . She was an artist with you, and somewhat deterrent. She has found a new purpose."

The day before the last Lessons were given, Maynard Holt, explaining to a friend the seven purposes, said: "Every human being who is for progress and construction serves one or more of these purposes. It is by them that what you know as human force is ultimately grouped for eternal advance. Our effort now is to unite all forces for Progress in conscious co-operation." After speaking of Germany's unity of purpose, he went on: "She is, and has been for years, the center of forces and purposes of disintegration in your life. She is, in theological parlance, the ally of his Satanic Majesty. We have learned here that there is no evil, per se. There is only purpose, constructive or destructive. . . . But the forces of disintegration are gathering for a battle of wits and morals, and we are emulating Germany in just one thing. . . . We are preparing. We want you to wake up and realize what is going on. We want every one of you to find and recognize not only your own purpose, but the other fellow's. Find out who is for progress, and who merely camouflages disintegration. Conscious co-operation of constructive purpose is warranted to beat the devil. He can't defeat it, nor yet delay it. (O) *That* is what it means to all of us. . . . Come on in. The water's fine!"

V

As has been said, our invisible friends have seemed somewhat hazy in their perceptions of time and place and of mundane details generally, and they have shown no inclination to concern themselves with our trivial personal affairs. When pressed for specific statements about small details, their replies have been sometimes in exact accordance with the fact as we have perceived it, sometimes not, but they have rarely diverged widely from the truth. In the larger matters directly related to spiritual unity and growth they have been correct, as when Mary K. explicitly stated, March 23d (already quoted), that the German offensive then in progress and up to that time successful would ultimately fail.

On one occasion, apropos of certain questions her husband had asked, Mary Kendal said: "We are not here to satisfy intellectual or any other kind of curiosity. If we were not sure you would use this information for construction, we wouldn't fuss about it—except you and I, Manzie."

Several times during March and April, however, Mary K. gave me correct and specific information about various minor affairs, and these incidents are mentioned here because I have been asked repeatedly whether such statements had been made and verified, rather than because undue importance is attached to them.

For example, hastening to an appointment one morning (March 29th), I carelessly left my muff in a taxicab. Discovering the loss an hour later, I telephoned to the cab company, to be told that no report had been received from the cabman, but that they would try to locate him at one of their various stands. It was arranged that I should call at their office for it late in the afternoon, had it been found.

During luncheon, which I took at a restaurant, Mary K. indicated that she had something to say, and on the back of an envelop wrote: "Your muff is found for you." Two hours later, when I reached home, the muff had been returned by the cabman.

Another incident, less accurate in detail, but substantially correct, concerned Mr. Kendal and my record-book. Having had, during his brief stay in New York, no leisure in which to read the record—which then contained only the genesis of this experience, Frederick's first interviews with his mother, and some messages from Mary Kendal not included in my letters to her husband—he had taken the book away with him (March 20th), and three or four days later I began looking for its return. When, on the 29th or 30th (exact date not noted), it had not arrived, I asked Mary K. whether she knew anything about it, and she replied that it had been sent and would probably reach me that day. At that time the record, wrapped and addressed, lay on his desk, where he had left it with instructions that it be mailed when he left home for the Easter week-end. It had been overlooked, and he found it there when he returned on the following Monday. Apparently Mary K. perceived only his intention and belief that it was on its way to me.

On the 1st of April she told me that a letter concerning these communications, then several days overdue, for which I waited with great anxiety, had at last been written.

"Really written?" I asked. "Or is this one of those successfully started things you regard as accomplished?"

"Really written."

At the same time she promised me other

letters, from persons specifically named, and gave me certain information concerning a member of the Gaylord family.

Two days later, when none of these letters had appeared, I said, "Where are those letters you promised me?"

"The letters are coming, fearful and wonderful messenger," she humorously assured me. "You have not made a ~~m~~ . . . ~~fr~~ . . . ~~friend~~ . . . ~~free~~ . . . fantom (O) friend in vain."

Laughing, I asked: "Is 'fantom friend' right?"

She said it was.

Half an hour later the long-delayed letter arrived, and as she had told me, it was dated April 1st. The other letters came later the same day, the one from Mrs. Wylie verifying the information already given by Mary K. about a member of her family.

On Monday, April 1st, I sent a copy of Frederick's recent interviews with his mother and sister to Mrs. Gaylord at K——, hoping that it might reach her by Wednesday morning. Wednesday night Mary K. told me that an expected letter from Mrs. Gaylord had not been written, adding: "She waits for the record." A week later, after a happy visit in K——, Mrs. Gaylord returned to her home and notified me that she had not received the manuscript from me. Fearing that it had been lost in the mails, I asked Mary K. about it, and was told that it would be received. This was repeated at intervals covering several days.

When, on Monday, April 15th, two weeks from the day it had been sent, it was missing still, I told Mary K. that it must have been lost.

"They shall have it soon," she said. "It is not lost, but delayed."

"Shall I make a duplicate for them?"

"You must trust us."

"You are positive that it will arrive?"

"Yes, it will."

It was delivered to Mrs. Gaylord the following day, April 16th.

On one occasion I asked Mary K. about a woman for whom I had been requested to arrange an interview with a person on the next plane, but about whom I knew nothing whatever.

"She is deterrent," was the reply, and during the subsequent interview, for the first time since the beginning of this experience, I encountered an individual whose outlook and desire was limited to the narrowly personal.

One of the most striking of these examples of specific information occurred on the night of Tuesday, April 2d, the day of the Senatorial elections.

Cass said: "Ask Mary K. whether she will answer a specific, mundane question for me." When she had written her name and indicated her willingness, he inquired: "Who was elected in Wisconsin to-day, Lenroot or Davies?"

"Are you there?" I questioned, when no reply came.

"Yes."

After another delay, when the pencil wandered lightly and aimlessly, she wrote: "Lenroot." Supposing that she had finished, I put the pencil aside, but she summoned me again, to add: "Lenroot elected by latest count. Close in some places. We consider him elected." Cass looked at his watch. It was five minutes past twelve.

The next morning our papers announced Mr. Lenroot in the lead, with final returns not yet received, and not until Cass reached his office did we discover how truly "exclusive" our information had been. He learned then that the suburban editions of several New York City papers, which probably went to press about the time we talked to Mary K., practically conceded the election to Mr. Davies, reporting him ahead by returns then available.

Of many other specific statements that were

either absolutely correct, or so nearly correct
that Mr. Kendal's theory of a difference of
perceptive method might easily account for the
error, one is notable. On Sunday, May 19th,
I asked Mary K. whether she could tell me
anything about the projected German drive.

"Yes. It will be fierce, but futile. All
forces here see her doom, and the war will last
only as long as unsupported human endeavor
can endure against eternal purpose. Germany
has no ally here. The forces that have impelled her for these many years are overpowered
by world-purpose, and have left Germany to
her destruction, while they prepare to destroy
the finest spiritual fruits of victory."

Similarly, while writing to friends at the
front of our entire confidence in the outcome
of the Picardy drive then in progress, May
30th, I paused to ask Mary K. whether she
had anything more to say about the war.

"Only that we are the victors. Germany
does not win this drive, either. Our forces
rally, and the end is near. Defeat this time
will leave them despairing and afraid."

To this Maynard Holt added, "All the forces
have withstood the blow and gather for the
final and decisive defeat of Germany."

VI

THE actual existence of intelligent, invisible forces, constantly doing battle for and against spiritual progress, through possession of what we are wont to call our souls, was at first difficult for me to accept literally, the idea being in direct opposition to my whole mental tendency. While the theory was interesting, it seemed hardly credible in its specific, individual application. However, I was soon given a manifestation of the strength and pertinacity of the disintegrating forces, which—although it ultimately strengthened my conviction, proving highly corroborative—threatened for a time to end this effort, as far as I was concerned.

The last two Lessons were given to me on the 12th of April, and it had been arranged that Mr. T——, the representative of a publishing-house, should come on the evening of the thirteenth for a demonstration of the communication with the next plane. From the day this arrangement was contemplated, frequent assertions were made under Mary K.'s signature, concerning Mr. T—— and his attitude toward this experience, many of which were afterward proved untrue, and all of which I doubted, notwithstanding repeated proofs, already quoted, of her general correctness of statement. Day by day these messages grew more confusing, and I less able to account for them by any theory then formed. That a deliberate "drive" by malign powers was in progress never occurred to me, and would have seemed too absurd to credit, even had I thought of it.

As there seemed to be no close tie between Mr. T—— and any of those from whom he had expressed a desire to hear, no great eagerness on either side to complete a circle of which each was a part, I felt that the interview might present difficulties not encountered before, and resolved to do no writing during the day, reserving my strength for the evening's work.

In the morning, however, I had occasion to ask Mary K. for some brief information. Beginning, as usual, with her signature—somewhat haltingly done—the pencil wrote quickly, but erratically: "Mr. Farrow is dead." This man is a business associate of Cass's, living abroad.

Startled, I thought I must have taken the message incorrectly, but it was repeated.

"Mr. Farrow is dead. Cass will hear later."
When I insisted that this could not be true,
it was reiterated. "Yes, he is here, and ḅ . . .
~~blon~~ . . . ~~latter~~ . . . bewildered. Mary K."

Our personal relations with Mr. Farrow,
while pleasant, have never been close, being
based entirely upon a business connection, and
my affections were in no way responsible for
my resistance to this announcement, nor would
our personal affairs have been in any way influenced by his death. But I did not believe it.

"Farrow is here with us. May . . . Mary
K." This signature was slow and irresolute,
beginning as Maynard and ending as Mary
K., but lacking the firmness of either—an indecision and inconsequence characteristic, I
have since learned, of disintegrating force in
these invasions.

"Was he killed in an accident?"

"No. Pneumonia. Maynard. Tell Cass."

"Shall I telephone to Cass now?"

"No. I am watching over him. Maynard."

The use of the word "dead" in this connection was surprising, since the whole trend of
former communications had been toward elimination of the idea of death. Once more I
asked Mary K. if they were sure there had
been no mistake.

"Yes. He is dead to your life."

"You mean Farrow of P——? Not his brother? Or his son?"

"Yes, P——. It is true. You will hear soon. Cass must go there."

I telephoned to Cass, saying nothing of this experience, and found him in good spirits, proving that he had not heard of Mr. Farrow's death. Returning to the pencil, I told Mary K. I did not believe the information was correct.

"Yes, he is dead. A telegram on the way to Cass. He will receive it soon. Before one o'clock."

Some time later, having heard nothing from Cass, I told Mary K. again that there had been a mistake.

"No, it is true. Mr. Farrow of P—— is here with us. Cass will know in a few minutes. He will telephone."

I warned her then that my faith in her veracity was at stake, and that while I could not doubt that Frederick, Mary Kendal, Maynard Holt, and others, had communicated through me, I could not take the responsibility of publishing anything she had told me unless I could trust her in all things, adding: "If this is not true how can I be sure that any of it is?"

"Mary K. It is true. Don't doubt."

I said I had no wish to doubt, but that un-

less this message came from some other than
Mary K., I could not believe her again, if it
proved, as I was sure it would, to be untrue.
I began to suspect that disintegrating forces
were at work.

"It comes from the constructive force. Be
confident. It perplexes you."

Later experience has taught me that while
either force may be in complete command at
moments, during these struggles for control,
not infrequently a message begun by one is
finished by the other. During the three days
of this first persistent attack, however, I held
no key to the mystery, and the occasional
clearly constructive and characteristic messages
from Mary K. and Maynard Holt merely added
to my bewilderment and dismay. Yet never
for one instant during those three days did I
accept the repeated statements of Mr. Farrow's
death as true. Weeks afterward, Mary K. told
me why I was not deceived.

Since that time, too, I have learned more
clearly to distinguish personality by the degree and quality of force applied to the pencil,
which varies greatly with individuals, though
it sometimes varies in the same individual at
different times. But in the first experience it
did not occur to me to apply that test of
identification.

All that Saturday afternoon the argument went on at intervals, I insisting that Mr. Farrow was not dead, the pencil reiterating that he was.

At two o'clock Maynard said: "Believe in us, Margaret. We can help you better." It is evident now that this referred to the conflict with the disintegrating force, but at the moment I misunderstood it and reminded him of the many specific and inaccurate statements made, during the past few days, regarding the man who was coming that evening by appointment, asking if this were more misinformation of the same sort, to which the reply was: "No, Farrow is here. He is dazed, but will be taken care of."

An hour later, I returned to the pencil, begging them to tell me, before definite information reached me from other sources, that there had been a mistake.

"Mary K. You must not doubt. We shall lose control of you if you do." When I said that what I sought was truth, she said: "I know, but you doubt our control, and weaken it."

"I also doubt my own correctness."

"You are correct." As, indeed, I was. Her message reached my consciousness.

At three o'clock the insistence that Mr.

Farrow was dead continued, and attempts were made to explain former inaccuracies, on the plea of a difference in plane, creating "errors in terms of finite space."

Shortly before five, it was said that Cass had received news of Mr. Farrow's death, and was on his way home. A few minutes later Mary K. warned me again.

"You must not doubt. . . . You can't be a messenger without faith."

"How am I to know when you are telling the truth and when it is error?"

"The truth is the truth, and you must learn to differentiate between the planes." I suspect that she intended the last word to be "forces," and that control was wrested from her before it was written.

Resenting the whole confused situation, and entirely unable to account for my conviction that this message was false, I said: "If Cass tells me, when he comes home, that Mr. Farrow is dead, I will believe anything you tell me in future. If he is not dead, I'll have nothing further to do with you or your book."

"Mary K. You will go on with our work. He is dead."

At this point, Cass arrived. He said that he had received neither letter nor cablegram from Mr. Farrow for ten days, although an expected and important letter from him was some time overdue. This seemed to lend color to the report of his death, but my conviction was unshaken.

From the beginning of these communications with the next plane, although at times excessively fatigued, I had enjoyed an increasing mental serenity, but with the first announcement of Mr. Farrow's death, this had given way to the peculiar nervous instability and apprehension invariably accompanying these mischievous invasions.

By night my mind was in a turmoil and my nerves on edge, my confidence shaken, my faith in the balance—which did not lessen the difficulties of an interview prompted chiefly by intellectual interest. Establishing connection with an unfamiliar personality is not easy, at best, and frequently some time is required to obtain free communication. On this occasion, instead of devoting the evening to perfecting one connection, several persons were called, all but one responding, and the messages, with one or two exceptions, were unsatisfactory. There were vain and fatiguing efforts to write a name unknown to any of us, and most of the efforts to obtain specific evidential data were unsuccessful. Whether this was due to my own lack of confidence, to interference by the enemy, or to the fact that at no time have the individuals communicating through me concerned themselves with personal and specific details—except occasionally, for my own greater conviction—I do not know.

At midnight, when this interview was over and we were alone, although wearied to the point of exhaustion, I asked again about Mr. Farrow, receiving the same reply, with a variation to the effect that the cablegram announcing his death had been delayed by the censor, and with occasional phrases of appeal and encouragement—merely intensifying my bewilderment—from Mary K. and Maynard.

"Are you sure you haven't been away and let in disintegrating forces?" I asked Mary K.

"No, we have been here. They can't touch your purpose. Don't fear. You will be perfectly reassured soon," was her reply, which, had we but recognized it, was an intimation that disintegrating forces had been in partial control in spite of all effort to overcome them.

Again I asked why the word "dead" had been used, and was told: "That is what the cable to Cass says." Which manifestly did not explain.

Sunday morning, Maynard Holt's familiar signature came at once, followed by a long, personal message to a friend who was present, steadily written, and pointed by an occasional characteristic turn of phrase, indicating a clear and uninterrupted connection.

When this had been finished, Cass asked, "Shall I go to the office for that cable?"

"It is not there."

"It's all a mistake?" I urged.

"Farrow is here."

But I knew he was not there. Had he been present in the flesh, I could not have been more certain that he had not left this plane.

All day we discussed the bearing of these persistent misstatements—provided they were misstatements—upon the experience as a whole, and I was oppressed, in addition to my personal disappointment, by a sense of my responsibility to those others to whom this new faith had brought active happiness and hope. I had arranged to go to L—— on the following Tuesday, to spend a few days with the Gaylord family; Mr. Kendal expected to arrive in New York a week or ten days later, anticipating further communication with his wife; and various other appointments were pending. But though I could neither question the authenticity of former personal communications, nor deny the constructive quality of the Lessons, I felt that I could not continue to act as intermediary if it were possible for persons like Mary K. and Maynard to lend themselves to this sort of thing, nor could I encourage others to hold a belief after it had become impossible to me.

In the afternoon, Mary K. told me to go to L—— as soon as possible. When we asked about Mr. Farrow, Maynard's signature preceded the message.

"He is here. Why don't you accept it?"

"I don't know why I can't," was my reply. "Why don't you convince my mind, as you have at other times? Why don't you make me feel it? I can't believe it's true."

"You have the statement of two friends."

"You've been mistaken before in specific statements."

"Only in those relating to dimensions of finite space, which we are unable to gauge accurately."

That evening, Mary K.'s signature came first. "You must see how foolish it was to mistrust us," the pencil wrote. "Mr. Farrow is here, and Cass will learn of it soon."

"Unless you take refuge again in that difference of plane," I commented, rather bitterly. "Why don't you remember it before, instead of after, the error it creates?"

"Because you should not distrust us."

"But why not encourage me to trust you by remembering that difference of plane in the first place?" I insisted. "Why be so explicit about things you know may be inaccurately stated?"

"I do not deceive you intentionally. We feel that a thing certain of accomplishment is done, and are frequently misled into premature statements by the strength of intention, or purpose, or movement in a given direction. We are accurate from our point of view, and not always able to gauge yours."

Admitting this to be conceivable, I said: "Now tell me about Mr. Farrow."

"Mr. Farrow is here with us. When Cass gets to the office in the morning he will find the truth." Again the signature was hesitating and indefinite, first Maynard, then Mary K. I felt that neither of them wrote it, but could not reconcile the frequent constructive statements, urging faith and continuance of this work, to destructive purpose, nor could I understand why, if Mary K. and Maynard were present, they did not warn me of false statements by malign forces, provided such were the case.

Monday morning, the situation was unchanged, save that the statements were slightly elaborated. Repeatedly I asked whether they were not confusing Mr. Farrow with some other member of his family, or whether they had accepted serious illness as death.

A curious statement followed this suggestion, under Maynard's signature. "Farrow is both here and there. He is here in essence, there in body. . . . He is both here and there for some time after death."

Immediately afterward, however, when I said that this sounded preposterous, Mary K.'s name was written, with: "Mr. Farrow is here. He is dead to you. Actually now dead. Go to L—— at once."

"I can't go to L——, with affairs in this state," I told her.

"You will know soon. Wait."

Maynard followed, with an appeal to "have faith," adding: "It will be clear soon."

This went on, at intervals, until after two o'clock, when I had promised an interview to a woman who had not visited me before. Fully resolved to tell her that I could take no messages for her, I made one last attempt to obtain the truth before her arrival—this time with partial success.

"Maynard. It is a mistake . . ."

At that moment, my guest arrived. I told her that I might be unable to get any satisfactory communications for her, but her daughter, who left this plane years ago, came at once, writing steadily and clearly, with the exception of one brief interruption. She told her mother of the seven purposes and their meaning, urging her, as had all the others, to put herself consciously in touch with constructive purpose, and to open her mind and spirit to those on the next plane who were eager to work with her.

When I was again alone, I returned to the pencil, which wrote quickly and strongly: "Maynard. It is a mistake about Farrow. The . . ." Here again the opposing forces evidently gained control. "Farrow here, but not your Farrow."

"Then why have you insisted that he was our Farrow?"

"He led us to think so."

I said with some emphasis that I wanted a better explanation than that.

"Maynard. You are messenger for us only if you trust us."

A fortnight later, after a second, similar experience, Mary K. told me, when I asked about this first confused period: "We had a terrific struggle for you then. We told you the truth, but the other forces controlled the pencil. . . . The forces of disintegration compelled us for the moment. We were not theirs, but they overpowered and used us."

Early in June, while preparing this manuscript, I asked her: "Was it you who wrote, 'You must not doubt. We shall lose control of you if you do'?"

"Yes. We were fighting for your faith."

"Can you tell me why you did not explain then—why you have never explained—that the enemy had control?"

"We have certain limitations in conflicts of this nature. . . . In actual conflict we can only affirm. Remember that. . . . When attacked by disintegrating force, the only way we can help you is to call to your purpose and to affirm our own. In your individual struggle we may not interfere, even when it concerns our work. You must believe or doubt, according to your own choice. . . . We cannot tell you that disintegrating forces threaten you, until you have recognized them. Then we can help you repel them. Always we call to you and try to encourage you. . . . You must make your own choice and your own deductions, and learn in that way to discriminate between the forces appealing to you. Details of your personal struggles may not be explained. They are your development."

Knowing nothing of all this in April, however, I insisted upon a detailed explanation of the Farrow mystery, and again the disintegrating forces played upon my doubt and bewilderment, elaborating excuses for the mistake, in Maynard's name.

Refusing to accept any of these ingenious but illogical assertions, I contended that they were unfair to me, having first specifically volunteered this erroneous information, which they now attempted to account for by obviously specious explanations.

"We volunteer information pertaining to the message we have for the world through you."

This, it will be perceived, was an affirmation indirectly disclaiming the Farrow messages, but I did not so recognize it, and reminded them that they had reproached me for not trusting them in this matter.

"You are logical within your limits," was Maynard's only reply to that.

"And you still expect me to go on with your work?"

"You have had many manifestations of our force," Mary K. returned. "Mr. Kendal will show you how this occurred."

When I mentioned, with some heat, that some one would have to show me, as they had asked me to shoulder a heavy responsibility in this matter, she said: "You are puzzled and frightened, but knowledge of our constructive work through you should decide your action."

Remembering how fear and grief and despair, in certain cases, and cynical indifference in others, had been banished from the lives of the men and women to whom these messages had come, I conceded the constructive work.

"Then come along and build. . . . You are unable to distinguish the difficulties under which we work. Many messengers have failed to convey the message we have tried to give. . . . Many mistakes happen with the best messengers."

"Was this my mistake?" I asked.

"No. You make only one mistake, so far. You shut us out by doubt. Don't doubt. We are all working for the same great end."

Eventually, although far from satisfied about the Farrow affair, I decided to go to L——, feeling that if disillusionment must come to the Gaylord family, it would better come now than later, but still hoping that some explanation would be given while I was with them. In this I was disappointed. Not until a fortnight later did I even begin to understand it. But after the first interview with Frederick at L——, I wrote Cass (April 17th): "If ever I had any doubts about the truth of this, they are gone! Somebody did something I don't understand, but this is *real*."

I have given this experience in some detail,

not only because it corroborates the statements that malevolent and crafty forces are about us, striving to thwart progressive effort, but because it seems also to offer at least a partial explanation of the inconsistencies and contradictions that long have baffled and discouraged investigators of psychic phenomena. Obviously, until the identity and character of the invisible communicating personality have been established and clearly recognized, and the purpose prompting the communication manifested through a series of experiments, it is unsafe to rely upon information received in this way. And it is equally obvious that forces of disintegration could scarcely find a more fruitful method of implanting in the human mind doubt and cynicism concerning the possibility of obtaining authentic and enlightening revelations from planes beyond, than by contradicting and confusing such messages, or by deliberately misleading the applicant for information.

Later experience brought further demonstration of the diligence of the sinister purposes, together with greater knowledge of ways to defeat them.

VII

BEFORE beginning the Gaylord interviews at L—— (April 17th), Mary K. asked me not to tell the family the details of the Farrow episode.

"Are you ever going to explain that clearly?" I asked.

"Not until you know more about these conditions."

That night, for the first time, I saw a photograph of Frederick. During the year of her grief and despair Mrs. Gaylord had been unable to bear the added poignancy of a portrait's suggestion, and only when I arrived, to manifest his actual presence in the family circle, was the hidden photograph—a singularly life-like and virile reproduction—brought to light.

"Hooray!" he began, after the customary signature. "Here we are again, all of us together at last! Dad! (O)" It will be remembered that this was the first time that either his father or his younger sister, Lois, had witnessed these manifestations. "You have been the one I wanted most, after Mother.

219

The girls I knew I could get sometime, for this is the future for everybody with purpose, and I knew they'd come to know me again soon. But you and Mother dearest I had to have (O) right now. You both need this knowledge and intercourse as much as I do. The fuller development that comes there with age and experience, and here—where there is no age except experience, makes me nearer to you and Mother in feeling and outlook than I am to the girls and Dick. Not that I am not one with all of you. But being here has showed me the reasons for the things—protective, over-seeing, far-seeing things—that you stand for, and have learned there through your experience in that preliminary life. So we are a lot nearer of an age than we used to be. Now we are off together again, and there is no reason, unless somebody backslides, why we can't keep step through the countless aeons of eternity. . . . Mother dearest, this time I sure am in. Thank you for putting me on the mantel. I like it. Coming home is lots happier business now. It used to make me sorry to see you all so sad. But this is bully! . . . Dad, look happy for the boy! He's here for keeps now."

Mr. Gaylord had generally spoken of Frederick, during his life here, as "the Boy." I had never heard him use any other name.

"Can you give your father the proof of your presence that you give me?" his mother asked. "Not only by writing, but by the feeling in his heart?"

"I will in time. Remember, he hasn't yet grown used to this communion. It hits everybody hard, at first, and this fluency is inconceivable to any one who has not seen and felt it at first hand. Give us time to get used to it, and Dad will be as fully in touch with me and my life as he ever was when I lived there. The shock and grief of my supposed departure are taking force from him still, but he'll see, just as you have, that I am the better and bigger for this one great experience, and that I never was so deeply and truly a part of his life. . . . Come on, now everybody talk! I sure do preach, but you called the turn the other day, Mother dearest. It's my job to get this across, first to you who are my own, and through you to every one you can reach. It's all our jobs."

Both Mrs. Gaylord and Lois had had some success in establishing communication with the next plane, through the pencil—obtaining detached words, and some names. And the former now asked: "Where were you Sunday? I tried to get you."

"I had a big job, attacking a pro-German

newspaper editor in South Africa. He didn't
give in, either, but we'll get him yet. He
doesn't fight openly. He poses as a Pharisee,
but he's really pro-German, and thanks God
he is like other Germans."

Lois asked whether there are any pro-
Germans where he is, and he replied that
disintegrating force is "pro- anything that
destroys."

During his last illness, one of his diversions
had been to plan with his father a long journey
they were to take together when he should be
convalescent. Now, after a pause, he wrote
slowly and distinctly, as if to emphasize the
deliberation of his intention:

"Dad, do you remember that trip we were
going to take? You take it with Mother some
day, and I'll go with you, and we'll do all the
things we planned. And I can tell you, if
you will just let me in and listen, all the things
you want to hear. We don't need a messenger, you and I, but as long as I can't get to
you any other way, I'll use one. I can help
you actually—physically, mentally, spiritually,
materially—as for so many years you helped
me. It was due to you and Mother that I got
such a good start here. Now I am here, it is
for all of us still, as it always was. But it's
my turn to lift a little. You carried me for

years. Let me come in again now, as a real, existing, active, growing force—your son, sir. wanting to be nearer and more intimately yours than ever. You go on and take our trip, and I promise I'll go with you. FREDERICK."

A little later, he said: "I wish there could be any way of showing you visibly the radiant force I am, now that we are all united. You have to be translated to this plane before you can understand what it means to be brought back into the family circle. Not all families, but ours. We are all of kindred purposes, and there's no separating us."

"I wish you'd do some of your 'stunts' for Father," Lois suggested.

"All right. If you want stunts, here is my best one." This was written briskly, upside down and backward from my position. "Dad, this is the way I wrote the letter to you and the girls. Here's another, with my love and greeting. I said I'd do this with trimmings. This is the beginning."

We gave him fresh paper, and he wrote rapidly, in winding circles, starting at the edge of the table and finishing at the center: "Now I'll do it this way, all around the family circle. All of you in, and I am not left out." Diagonally across the whole in bold script, "FREDERICK."

In moving the paper again, it was torn a

little. Mr. Gaylord made some suggestion as to the way it should be handled, and Lois humorously complained that he was "always interfering with other people's purposes." Beginning at the upper right-hand corner of the table, Frederick wrote along the edges, and then in circles toward the center, as indicated in the diagram:

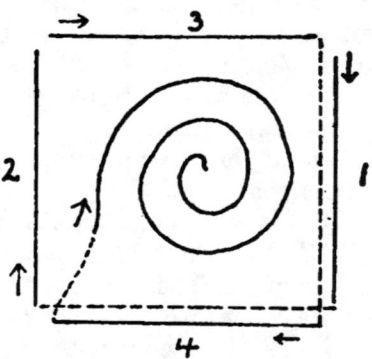

"Don't you mind, Dad. Let them laugh. You and I will be laughing at them presently, from all four points of the compass." Again his name was signed diagonally across the whole.

"I always did like circuses, and I can be a four-ringed one now, all by myself, if I have a sympathetic audience," was his next achieve-

ment, done once more in circles from edges
to center, but this time his name was signed
in the center, in small script, surrounded by a
flourish.

When again a clear surface offered, he drew
a large circle around the edge of the table—
the symbolism of which, curiously, occurred
to none of us until the next day—and then ran
to the center, to circle toward the edge:
"All of us together again, and all being happy
in the consciousness that this is real and
eternal union, and that from now on we are
going to keep our family circle intact."

Some one suggested that unquestionably he
was keeping his promise to "do it with trimmings," and in an intricate pattern, impossible
to describe clearly, he replied: "Sure! I'm
doing all the trimmings I can think of, and
after a minute or two I'll think of more."

By this time the astonishment and curiosity
aroused by these performances had perceptibly
lowered the emotional pressure, and the interview again proceeded more normally.

Not unnaturally, in this first family reunion
Frederick's messages were chiefly personal. Frequently, in pauses, he made enthusiastic little
circles, as has been his custom from the first,
and I asked him whether it was the circle of
infinity, all-inclusive.

"Yes, partly. Put out all disturbing factors and all forces of disintegration, add more to eternity and infinity—and that is the circle."

"Good night," he said, a little later. "I'll stay here to-night and as long as Margaret stays. You'll talk often, won't you?"

The next night, he began with a suggestion that the rest do the talking, adding: "I'll listen and answer questions." After some discussion of purpose, in its personal application, and inquiries concerning other members of the family on his plane, Mr. Wylie asked whether his grandfather could talk to him in this way.

"I can get him, I think, by to-morrow," Frederick replied. "He's sheltering a lot of poor, undeveloped wretches who have come out of conditions not making for fitness or growth. He teaches, and urges, and offers them opportunity, and is too busy and helpful to come away often."

After this had been written, I was told that this man, during his earthly life, had devoted time and money to providing opportunity for others; never offering charity, but building roads that the unemployed might have work, exchanging some commodity needed by a poor man for some other of which he had enough and to spare, and always encouraging his less fortunate fellows to retain and develop their self-respect.

Of another on his plane, now a healer, Frederick said: "I haven't seen him. Every healing force here, as with you, is occupied with war-stricken forces. They come so dazed, and sometimes terrified—and almost always startled, if they come from battle. And all our healing forces are required every minute."

This reminded Mrs. Gaylord of an experience of her own, a few days before, when her pencil had written detached words, suggestive of battle. "Lost . . . many lost . . . another dead . . . shot . . ." etc. She asked whether this came from a friend, and was answered in the negative. To her inquiry, "Did you live here?" the reply was: "Near." She asked for the name, and it was written clearly, "K——." A few days later the name of Lieutenant K——, of a neighboring city, headed the American casualty list.

"K—— caught his one chance before his consciousness dimmed," Frederick commented. "He is now too bewildered to talk. Just after what people who don't know call death, there is a moment of singular clarity and vision. He happened to catch you in that moment."

We fell to wondering, then, whether these messages could be flashed to us from a distance, or whether the person communicating must be present, and I asked Frederick whether he could send me a message from a distance.

"No, but we travel in a flash."

We who had had some experience in receiving these communications spoke of the fear we all had lest we might unconsciously influence the pencil, at times, to write our own imaginings.

"You people have such a fear of imagining things that you shut out a lot we try to tell you," Frederick interpolated. "We can't get through doubt, bitterness, resentment, or selfish grief. Fear can be conquered, but doubt shuts the door in our faces. Please relax a little of this too rigid vigilance, and at least entertain the idea we are trying to put over."

"Do I shut things out by too much vigilance?" I asked.

"You bet you do! But you do it for the best of reasons. You can't take chances of giving the wrong message."

To a question about the desire of others on his plane to communicate with those here, he replied: "They are all eager to get in touch, just now. Every one of us here is pulling every thread of connection he can there, because this is a critical time and because never before in the world's history have so many people been reaching out for the thing that means co-operation and progress, in the biggest and broadest sense, if we can only reach them and convince them that we are all working together, and that we here can help if they will let us."

Mr. Wylie spoke of some one whose "make-up," he thought, might enable him to receive these communications.

"Make-up has a lot to do with it," Frederick returned, "but the peculiar quality of following accurately a thought put forth by a force so subtle that science has failed to detect it is a thing that none of you recognize until it has demonstrated itself."

Some one asked about a prominent politician, whom Frederick had known well in this life, and he replied: "—— is working his way back to a place in the forces of Production. He had a great opportunity, and used it for personal ends, and now he is learning how to use it for Progress. He is not destructive, nor even deterrent. He is a fine force, delayed a little."

"Have you ever seen my mother and father?" Mr. Gaylord asked, thereby eliciting the most rapidly written communication—with the possible exception of one coming the next night—that I have ever taken, the force moving the pencil being so strongly applied, at moments, that the instrument was almost pulled out of my fingers.

It should be explained that in this appeal to his father Frederick was addressing neither reluctance nor doubt, but a certain mental tensity, resulting from deep emotion, deeply repressed.

"Yes, I had Grandmother at Mrs. Z——'s one day," he began. "She is very anxious to talk to you, but she has gone on to a life, or a plane, beyond the one I am on, and I can't always reach her. I hope to get her some time before Margaret goes home. . . . She never wholly left you, any more than I have. She tried for years to tell you she was there, and she wants to come back as soon as possible and tell you herself that there is no death, no separation, no cause for pain, or grief, or fear, or sadness of parting, except as it is made in the hearts of those who do not know the truth.

"We are nearer to you than you are to each other, Dad, and we can prove it, if you will let go of yourselves and take hold of us. We want to come to you. We do come to you. We try and try to tell you that there is nothing to grieve about, nothing to dread. Only love, and hope, and growth, and beauty of completer union. But we can't do it alone.

We must have a free heart, a free mind, a free hope to come into. Give us that, and we will show you that we are more truly your own—not your own flesh and blood, but your own purpose and force, which was one in the beginning, and will inevitably be one in the end. We want to make it one now. Don't you, Dad? Won't you try to let the bars down and take us in? We'll come, and we'll all be happier than you've ever been in all your life yet, because the Eternal Purpose is Unity, and we can begin it right here and now, if you there will join us and be part with us, as we with you, of the glorious and happy and (O) irresistible movement toward the great end—which, after all, is not an end, but an eternal and infinite growth toward bigger things.

"It is a big gospel we are giving you, sir; a man's gospel; a gospel of hope and beauty and construction. And I am asking you to let me come in again to your every-day life, to let the dread and misgiving and unhappiness go, to think of us here—all of us who are yours —as still yours, still with you, still loving and working and hoping with you and for you; and if you can do that, I promise you we shall all be happier than any of us have ever been before.

"You see, sir, we are all of the forces of

Progress. We are all for Light, and Building, and Justice, and Truth, and when one of us holds back we are all held back. This is the first time it has been possible to tell you all this. This is the first time we have been able to reach you freely, in a way you could not mistake. But the people who have preached the gospel of happiness as a curative force have not been entirely wrong. They have not been wholly right. But the forces here cannot possibly affect a tense and resisting mind as they can a relaxed and receptive one. And the forces here are potent and eager and ready. You know that must be true, because I am one of them, and the only change in me—absolutely the only one, Dad—is that I have left the limitations of the flesh behind and grown in perception and knowledge. I am the same Boy,[1] plus the better things, and minus the limitations.

"Grandmother is the same, too—plus. She is sweeter, finer, broader, more loving, than when you knew her. Just as she was, but expanded, irradiated, deepened. That's all that death means, so you see it isn't death at all, nor separation, nor anything but beauty, and

[1] Later developments make it seem probable that this was an attempt to write the familiar diminutive for which his father afterward asked, and that my "too rigid vigilance" shut out the suggestion.

greater love, and wider opportunity, and higher ideals to live to.

"This is what we want to share with you. We can, now. You can have a little of our knowledge, while still in that preliminary life. You can help us and yourselves by realizing and living the purpose that is ours. You have always lived it, but you haven't always recognized it. Do that, recognize it, recognize us, let us in as recognized and essential parts of your life and hope and happiness, and I shall not need to tell you that this is a true gospel. You will have proved it for yourself.

"Your son always,

"FREDERICK."

We were all deeply moved. After a little, Mr. Gaylord asked: "Is there anything more?"

Frederick began making circles, and his mother said: "He's so happy!"

"Happy isn't the word for it! I'm personified radiance and bliss! There isn't anything more to-night, except my love to all of you, always—and to-morrow, and the next day, and all the days to come, we are reunited and indivisible. That's enough, isn't it, sir? Good night. FREDERICK."

VIII

THE next day, that grandfather for whom Mr. Wylie had asked came briefly, discussing purpose, like the rest.

"I didn't half understand my own impulses there," he said, "but I know now that the best thing a man can do for other men—and for himself, too—is to give them a chance to develop whatever is in them. Sometimes it isn't much, from the point of view of the intelligent man, but the fact remains that it is force, and the more quickly it is developed the more quickly the sum of the whole will be raised."

He closed more personal assurances by saying: "There may be no way to put it into words, but you may be sure I am watching, and helping, and being helped, too, by your reaching toward our common purpose."

When Frederick had taken over the pencil again, Mrs. Gaylord spoke of the long message to his father the night before, to which he replied: "It was only a beginning. This thing we have to tell you can't be given, nor yet accepted, in a day or a month. That letter last night was a sort of foreword, just to get us all started even. The proof of the pudding is coming later."

Some more or less personal discussion followed, during which Mr. Gaylord asked whether certain arrangements he contemplated making were wise.

Frederick replied that they were, as far as he could see, adding: "This is hardly a time for making permanent arrangements, for while the end of the war is certain, the economic conditions with you, following the war, are impossible now to foresee. We have no way of knowing how that struggle between labor and capital, power of foundation and power of development, will end. That is one of the reasons we are so eager to get all forces for true progress united now. There are thousands of laboring men misled. Get them in for our work. There are hundreds of employers ignorant or indifferent. Turn them out."

Mr. Gaylord, who had not at that time read the Lessons carefully, interpreted this as championship of the cause of labor as opposed to capital. Some one else suggested that every one, employer or laborer, who was not for united progress, should be "turned out."

"Sure," Frederick answered. "Turn out the unions, as they work now. Get in unity, regardless of class."

When Mrs. Gaylord inquired about a member of her own family, he replied: "He has gone on, and I haven't seen him. To some of us here there comes a lessening of interest in your life, and an intensified feeling of the importance of work beyond your plane. He has this interest, I hear, and very rarely comes back now. There is a lot I want to tell you some time about the differences and conditions of the many planes, but I can't do it now. The first work of those of us who have still close ties there is to give you all we can of the possibilities and meaning of the life you live. Some day I'll tell you what I can of the life ahead, which as yet I only aspire to."

"I suppose there's no use asking whether you inhabit space, or planes, or stars?" Lois inquired.

"There are things that I can tell you later about those matters of plane and future progress," he said, "but there is so much that is more imperative now that I am told not to tell more, at present, than the immediate needs of your life require."

"Do you feel any depression, when you realize the immensity of the universe and the smallness of each individual?" was the next question.

"That's a thing you've got to learn. There is no force that is not true force, and no atom so small that its weight doesn't count. If one atom is for destruction, that means two atoms lost to construction, the one that is against us and the one that balances it here, without any forward movement."

"Have you seen my father?" Mr. Gaylord asked.

"No. He is a healer now, and has come back from the plane beyond to help the newly arrived find their balance. I have tried to get in touch with him, but he is busy and I haven't yet met him, but still hope to. Few come back for any work here, and their greater knowledge makes them very much in demand, just as a great surgeon is with you in times like these."

Again the talk turned into more personal channels, and Mr. Gaylord asked a specific question, affecting future arrangements.

"... Your choice will be influenced, probably, by many considerations, as choice must always be in your life. ... I can influence you in ways I can't define in words, but I can't properly tell you how to choose—as you know better than I. You taught me that, and it's true.

Every fellow on his own feet. . . . Not that I'm not eager to help, sir. You understand that, don't you? But the way I can help most is by a close and constant association and suggestion, that still stops short of definite expression of choice for you. That is your privilege. Mine is to help you see the way more clearly."

"Do you know what we are thinking, at all times?"

"Not always. We read most of the thought of the sympathetic forces, and some of everybody's. I can't always answer the thought I read, though I can sometimes. But Margaret keeps up such a stiff guard, I can't always get over a thing she doesn't know is asked."

I said I was sorry for that, and did not understand it, as I thought I had lowered all guards as far as he was concerned.

"You can't understand all the barricades— and the limitations, too—of consciousness. Sometimes I sneak one through on you, but you are from Missouri, all right! You want to see the works before you admit the applicant."

After dinner, we talked a little about the publication of these communications, and of the extent to which personal messages should be quoted.

As soon as we gave him opportunity, Frederick said: "You people can't guess what it means to hear you talking about me, in the old, happy way. I've missed myself terribly, you know. . . . You've been talking about the book. If you'll permit a suggestion from me, the plan of copious quotation from all the interviews that have bearing on the big message, as well as some characteristic extracts from the more personal messages, under initials frankly substituted for real ones, is to my notion the way to do it. . . . A good deal of what we have been allowed to say was because this message was given through Margaret, and the rest of us have told things that illumine and carry on the message for the world. We have all wanted you of our own to know these things, but the channels through which this has come to her have been chosen for her fuller conviction, and to enable her to deliver this with greater force."

In this connection, it is interesting to note that in every instance when messages of importance have come, it has been during intercourse primarily requested by those gone before, who have asked me to send for the person here through whose co-operation the freest communication could be established—Frederick writing more fluently to some member of his family than to me alone, Mary Kendal to

Mansfield, David Bruce to his wife, and so on. Conversely, interviews arranged at the instigation of persons on our own plane have been generally without satisfactory result.

"We who can tell it clearly, and whom she can absolutely identify," Frederick went on, "have had extraordinary fluency, and almost unlimited authority to speak. We have spoken to our own, and through them to all who will listen. Keep the personal part of all we have said as sacredly to yourselves as you like, but my own desire is that the parts of my messages that will carry conviction or comfort to people suffering in ignorance of all this may be given to them through you—as your faith and conviction will lead you to do, I know—not in your name or mine, but in the spirit of light, healing, and progress we all serve."

When this was construed as an intimation that he did not want his name used, he returned: "I have no slightest objection. I have only a feeling that this personal revelation belongs to you. Use it as you choose. I do not ask anything, except that you share its essence with those who suffer as you have suffered. Give them what will relieve them, and do it as you think best."

At this point, the question of publication was dropped, though he returned to it the next day. A short pause followed. Then the touch on the pencil changed, Frederick's bolder writing being succeeded by a smoother, more flowing, and exceedingly rapid script, in a message to Mr. Gaylord from his mother, for whose early death he had never ceased to grieve.

"—— dear, this is Mother.

"Frederick told me I could reach you at last. I have had always the greatest desire to touch you, to tell you that your mother could not leave you, could not cease to love you, could not leave off watching over you, hoping for you, guarding your highest hopes and ideals. To have known the darkness that fell upon you, and to be unable to lighten it, or to soothe your anguish, made me as sad as one can be in this fine and everlastingly expanding life. I knew that you must some day come back to me, and into full knowledge of all that eternal life means, so I could bear it.

"You have been always a joy and a source of great happiness to me, in your splendid adherence to the things we know now to be the first and fundamental principles of life. We did not know, when I was with you, all the wonders and beauties of the eternal life we talked about. We thought heaven was quite different from this. But it is heaven,

in a much higher and finer way than anything we dreamed of then, and to be able to
come back to you now—to my boy, through
his boy—and tell you all this, is almost as
wonderful and blessed to me as it is to you.

"I have gone on to a life and a work I cannot easily explain to you now. I have lost
touch with the material things of your life.
But you, your purpose, your achievement of
force, the love you have never ceased to give
me, the love with which you bless and are
blessed by your family—all these things I know,
dear, and have always known.

"For so long, I tried to tell you not to grieve.
We have been so close together, in the ways
that are real and infinite. Never grieve again,
dear son, for any loved one coming to this
happy life. We do not leave you. We do
not part in any way, except the way of flesh.
We are happy, but can be so much happier if
you know us with you and of you, and if you
can come to us in confidence and love and
conviction of our life, as we never cease to go
to you.

"Your father wanted me to tell you this is
from him as well as from me. He is doing
a great work and cannot come to you now, but
he knew that I should soon come to say this,
and he wants you to know that he, too, is

happier in your growing knowledge of our unceasing life, and unceasing love, and unceasing upward growth.

"Your family are all dear to us as part of you, and therefore part of us. It is a light increasing the light in which we dwell, to be at last in this close communion with you. I will come again some time—many times—and I want you always to think of me as loving you, keeping watch over you, and living in you and yours.

"Frederick is splendid. You know that. Please be as sure that I am—and your father, too—always so full of happiness in the thought and knowledge of you and your love.

Your loving

MOTHER."

IX

"I AM with all of you as I never could be before," Frederick said, the next day, "because until we are realized and recognized the communion can't be complete. Now I can tell all of you lots of things you can get without words or messenger. Sometimes you will know they are my suggestions, sometimes you won't. But the fact that I am closely and intimately in touch with you is the important thing for all of us. The recognition of my definite suggestion will come later, when you are more accustomed to all this and have learned the little signals by which I identify myself to you."

"Can you tell us what those signals are?" some one asked.

"They are like the force I am, too subtle for scientific analysis or description, but you'll know them, all of you. This thing can't be developed in a minute, you know. Wait, and watch, and let the bars down, and you'll know me when I come, in a comparatively short time."

"Can you tip tables with us?" Lois inquired.

"Yes, probably; but that's a clumsy way of doing it. Some of you can run a planchette. None of you are likely to get anything like this. . . . This fluency of reception is hardly to be expected. We can talk, however. . . . You can always get me, for the essential intercourse, and somehow we'll get it across."

"I want you to give your father something like the 'stop—look—listen' reminder to me," his mother said.

"All right; but I can't do it in cold blood. Let me cogitate, and I'll try to think up a password that can't fail to accomplish the desired effect. You and Dad are the same purpose in essentials, but your force is differently applied and can't be approached in the same way."

"How far down in the scale does the possession of a soul go?" Mr. Wylie asked, presently. "How about animals?"

"There is no such thing as soul, in that sense. All purpose is force. All force personified is individuality. All individuality is eternal. The development is unequal. The undeveloped force finds quicker development here. But the force that has been developed to a point of intelligence in your life, and is not actively put to work, goes down in the scale, is deterrent, and has to work just as hard to get back as the force that never has developed at all."

"Where does the force animating babies come from?" I asked. "What was little Dick before he was little Dick?"

"That's what I want to explain, if I can. The force that manifests itself in animals is a grade higher in force than the vegetable manifestation, and that higher than inanimate stone and metal. The force of an animal comes here, to swell the forces that become individual and human through birth, but individuality begins with human consciousness. All force that is not human may eventually become human, but there is no persistence of individuality until birth as a human and more or less productive force begins it. Animals do not produce anything but their kind. Only man creates, and that is the eternal attribute."

"Is there a struggle between purposes to enter a new-born human?"

"Many purposes are latent in every human being from birth. None is in absolute possession. Life on your plane is one perpetual struggle between the eternal warring purposes. No newly born child has chosen. The training of a child should, from the first, be a preparation for battle, for daily—almost hourly— choice. Diligence, vigilance, purpose to work

unceasingly and against all disintegrating influences, determination to construct and to
progress in spite of anything, mental, moral,
physical, or material—these are the essential
things in training a child to live forcefully and
eternally."

"What becomes of babies who die at birth?"

"They have undeveloped personalities and
are developed here. We have strong forces of
Light and Truth devoted to their teaching."

"When a man is consciously determined to
construct, is he ever overcome by disintegrating forces?"

"Sure thing he is, if he doesn't fight. Sometimes he sways and recovers. Read the Lessons. They'll tell you more every time you
read them. They come from General Headquarters. . . . The arousing force of this message is to be measured by conviction manifested in action. Again you are respectfully
referred to the Lessons."

"It doesn't seem fair that physical and
nervous conditions should affect one's ability
to resist or receive the forces," Lois mentioned.

"It doesn't. You just think it does. The
forces of construction are always eager to
come in. The thing you call nervous exhaustion generally comes from yielding to forces
of disintegration. A person yields to one or

more of them, and then is sorry for himself because some doctor doesn't rout them. What he needs is to buck up and kick them out himself." Evidently he referred here to the nervous disorders arising from mental disturbances, for the next day he emphasized the government of physical forces by physical laws.

It was suggested that while many nervous disorders might be controlled in their incipiency by the person suffering from them, they eventually get beyond his control, and Frederick replied: "You think so; but there's always force where there's personality, and if it can just be put up to you, by yourself or another, that the choice in the end is yours and nobody's else, you can help yourself. In the end, you help yourself, anyhow, unless you slide back to protoplasm of purpose. Get busy and buck up, or backslide and slump. It's up to every fellow for himself, and every one who slips back impedes the way for somebody else."

In the talk following this, some one spoke of the constant teaching of brotherhood and regard for one's neighbor as a vicarious gospel.

"Not vicarious," Frederick corrected. "It is not vicarious to give the other fellow a chance. No man is his brother's keeper. No man has a right to impede construction, unless he's destructive. But it's every personality developed to its highest that makes the strong constructive army. The weak should have a chance to develop, but no strong force should yield its purpose. Nothing vicarious about that. Just common sense and good organization."

Mr. Gaylord—the successful head of a large manufacturing concern—asked, with a twinkle: "Can you successfully run a business in accordance with the principles laid down in these Lessons? Before you answer, I want to say that I believe it can be done."

"You're right, Dad. It can't be done easily, nor quite consistently, at present, because of the complexity of modern business conditions. You are all bound to some extent by association with some one else, whether by a man, a directors' board, an association, or a contributing concern. These all limit, to a certain extent, your freedom of action; but fundamentally the principle is practicable, and can gradually be put into consistent practice by uniting with those of your own purpose, instead of with those who seem expedient."

That evening, Mrs. Wylie said that the repeated assertions of invisible forces of construction and of destruction, alertly striving to influence us, reminded her of the old theories of guardian angels and possessing devils.

I think it was that night, too, though I made no record of it at the time, that Mr. Gaylord said, when Frederick's good night had been followed by his customary signature: "I wish he'd sign the name I used to call him by." Efforts to obtain it then, however, were unsuccessful.

The next day—the last of my visit—Frederick said of a man of whom we had been talking: "He hasn't just found himself yet, but he will. He likes to produce some things, and he will respond to the higher call to build for the higher end. You can all help him, and yourselves, and our whole purpose, by calling to the latent builder in him. He wants to come in, but doesn't know just where to start. . . . More effort, more concentration, more force applied for purpose, is the thing to strive for first. I can't tell him how to build. That's for him to choose. . . . You can build together. Each of you helping the other, each of you bringing effort, willingness, perception, force of various kinds. But first and foremost, devotion to the purpose of progress, regardless of intervening difficulties and discouragements. Habit is strong in every human force. Remember that, and watch—watch for the little masquerading devils of destruction. They are clever and subtle, and come in plausible guise.

Kick them out and work. . . . You said this sounded like the old stories of possession by devils, Sis. It's not that. The devils of old possessed a man in spite of himself. The forces of destruction govern him only when he permits them to. He can always be constructive, if he will. He may do no more than carry bricks to the mason, but still he builds. The man who has great opportunity must use it greatly. The little chap can use only the force he has. Thus endeth this preachment."

Lois asked whether he had been present at a moment when several members of the family had been in great physical danger, and he replied that he had come at once, from a great distance, in response to a summons from a force "that is always with you when I am not."

"There is always a connecting force between you and the free forces here," he explained. "We are always in touch that way. That is equally true of the forces for destruction. The greater forces for good or evil can be instantly summoned to reinforce your choice."

This led to a discussion of prayer, in which certain members of our group had lost faith.

"You can always summon help, if you call the (O) eternal constructive forces to build with you," he told us. "But most people

pray for physical or material aid. Physical
forces follow physical laws. Forces of eternity
affect them to some extent, but do not govern
them. Prayer with other people is a sort of
lying down on the Infinite and giving up personal effort. The prayer that is most truly
and promptly answered is the one that begins
and ends with a determination not to yield
to weakness, or fear, or the other disintegrating powers. Prayer implies an open mind, and
is too often made with a closed one. Not wilfully closed, but fearfully, and therefore not
truly open."

"Physical forces, Mother, were too much
for my physical resistance," he said, when she
spoke of her effort to hold him here. "No
amount of prayer, or influence of the forces of
eternal progress, could affect that, beyond the
extent to which it was affected. That is the
reason it was a long fight. The forces helped
all they could. But the physical thing is a
minor thing, after all. The eternal thing is
all that really counts. And to be able to put
you, whom I love so much, in touch with the
eternal while still in that preliminary life, is
worth all that I—and you—went through to
make it possible. To be able to pass on this
knowledge to that life of yours is worth anything."

"Isn't the time coming when we shall be able to control our physical condition better than we do now?" Mrs. Wylie asked.

"Yes, the mind—and what we call force in the eternal sense—has great influence over personal physical force. It performs no miracles, but prevents much yielding to what is really the forces of destruction, trying to hamper and delay accomplishment of any constructive kind. . . . The forces of disintegration are the busy boys, and it takes force and purpose and struggle to keep them out."

"Is our decision to use your first name in the book right?" his father asked.

"Yes, sir. I am very happy about that. It will identify me, and therefore the message, to many people I should like to reach personally, and will not identify you to the public at large. I should not like to have Mother and the girls annoyed by publicity, but that was for you to choose. The message, as you know, is important and general. But to a lot of fellows I want to reach, Frederick will carry where Z. X. would fail to convince. . . . Your attitude about the book pleases me, too. . . . You and I both know the force of the primitive masculine feeling that a man's family is his own, and its affairs private and personal. This time, the personal affair is also the eternal affair, vital and illuminating. And the fact that I have been one of the channels through which this came, that it was the search for me that made Margaret begin this work, must not be confused in anybody's mind with the fact that the message is more than a message—it is a revelation. For that reason, you and I both will gladly sink the personal reluctance and remember the purpose we serve."

A long pause ensued, while we sat soberly about the table, waiting. Then some one suggested that perhaps he wished us to ask questions.

"All I want is to talk like folks to the family," he announced, with a force and rapidity amounting to emphasis. "For the love of Mike, stop thinking of me as different, and translated, and serious, and solemn! I do preach a lot, I admit. That's for reasons you know. But I'm just as fond of a joke as I ever was, and I refuse to be set aside as a superior being! Come on, now, count me in as the Boy, and out as a thing to be treated with solemn reverence! I'm myself, and I want it recognized!"

After this, the talk drifted, much as it might have done had he returned visibly after a long absence, touching here and there.

Presently Lois asked, referring to a friend

in Europe: "Did you know H—— was married? And to an American woman?"

"No, I didn't know that. He should marry a free force, like an American girl. He was too blamed medieval in his feeling about females. We are all a bit inclined that way, we men, but American women are doing a lot to free force, the world over. They are more nearly free in purpose than any other women in the world, more truly individuals—when they don't abuse it, and turn into dolls. American girls help women everywhere. They don't stand for any harem stunts. H—— will learn a lot of things he needs to know, if she's the real thing."

Concluding a long reply to a personal question of his father's, he said: "Know that I am enjoying every pleasure you take, doubly, once for you and twice for myself. There's your watchword, Dad! One for myself, and two for the Boy. Remember that every time you are worried, every time you are tempted to overwork, every time you put off physical repairs, every time you feel depressed, every time you need rest and relaxation and pleasure, every time you play with Mother and the girls, every time you renew your fellowship with other men—always remember: One for myself, and two for the Boy."

That evening, Mrs. Gaylord said that she had received a message about a relative in the West, purporting to come from her brother on the next plane, which she thought was not true, but one of her daughters told her that a letter received the night before had verified it.

"Mother dearest, all messengers have that trouble," Frederick warned her. "There are certain things concerning details of your plane, that will come to you through forces around you, that get confused in transmission. That's as near as I can come now to explaining what happens. Some day, I can perhaps tell you more about it. But don't let that disturb or discourage you. The explanation is as natural as a deflected ray of light, or an electric current grounded.[1] It is a part of the conditions under which we work with your plane, and is never encountered regularly or continuously. Certain detached experiences of that sort come to every messenger. This one you mention was not one of them, but I tell you this now, because the experience may come to any of you, including Margaret, any day. The current gets mixed. That's the best way I can express it. But it doesn't persist for any length of time."

We talked about the force moving the

[1] Short-circuited?

pencil. Mr. Gaylord asked whether I wrote the words, after receiving the message through my mind, and I replied that the force, on the contrary, seemed to be applied to the pencil from without—sometimes above my fingers, sometimes below them—my only participation being to hold the pencil upright and to follow its movement. Mrs. Wylie mentioned the theory that the message comes through the subconscious mind, the muscles of the hand supplying the motive power. We asked Frederick whether he could tell us anything about it.

"The subconscious mind is like the battery," he said, slowly, "but the connection is made through the hand. The motive power for the pencil does not come, as scientists claim, from the subconscious mind, but from the subtle force I mentioned, put into connection with the hand by certain sympathetic and sensitive conditions of the subconscious mind. The comparison is not exact. The force is not electric, and has certain definitely distinctive qualities not to be expressed in any terms now familiar to your plane; but in time words will be found—or coined—to express this connection."

Some weeks afterward, Mr. Kendal obtained a little additional information about this unknown force from his wife.

In endeavoring to establish communication with Frederick, through a pencil, one of his sisters had been overwhelmed by insistent, and frequently unknown, personalities seeking expression, and had had some rather violent and annoying manifestations of the force they employ.

"You mustn't do too much of this writing stunt," Frederick now advised her, "unless you give up a lot of other things. You can't burn your candle of force at both ends. Margaret gave up a lot of outside activities long ago. You are sensitive, and could do this in time very freely, but the receptivity is decidedly a strain upon the messenger at best, and if any amount of writing is to be done, you can't do other things, too." After mentioning that she would probably be beset by "any number of yearning forces," he added: "So either say 'not at home' to anybody but Uncle J—and Bud . . ."

I halted the pencil, supposing that he had intended to write either Boy or Brother, and that there had been a mistake in transmission.

Lois glanced at the sheet, and ejaculated: "Buddie!"

"That's the name I've been waiting for!" her father exclaimed.

The pencil then went on, completing the

name as if no interruption had occurred: ". . . die, or give up other things, or quit."

Afterward, when it had been explained that certain members of the family had called Frederick Buddie, Bud, or Buzz, variations of Lois's baby attempts at Brother, he added: "I've been trying to get that through, but the Missourian held me to known names."

At first, names came to me with little difficulty, but latterly—possibly beginning with the Annie Manning episode—I have been generally unable to transmit them. Some one asked Frederick the reason for this.

"Because names are specific," he said. "She knows my name. She knew I had a special name, besides. But while an idea expressed in familiar words can be transmitted, however unfamiliar the idea, the definite and specific spelling of an unfamiliar name is very difficult to get through, especially if the messenger is a little nervous about it, or constantly alert for possible mistakes. We can sometimes get it through, as I did this, in a rush of other stuff."

[A few days later, when I was very tired, receiving with difficulty, and therefore questioning every statement made through the pencil, Mary K. said: "You are the most mentally . . . el . . . elas . . . el . . . elastic is not the word. Means elastic and masterful . . . impregnable messenger I ever tried to work through. . . . That is the reason names are almost impossible to send through you. You try to get them, but the almost invincible character of your mental resistance to deception makes it difficult for us to penetrate where a doubt exists in your mind. A name is specific to the highest degree, and resistance, however unconscious and unrecognized, prevents its free transmission."]

"You will come again, won't you?" Frederick asked, as the hour of my departure approached. "I have had a bully time talking to the family, and I can do better work now, because they are all happier, and all with me in conscious purpose. It's true that every bit of conscious co-operation with us helps us, as well as you. So that 'One for myself and two for the Boy' is not bunk, Dad. It's the real thing, for both of us."

With a final brief message to every member of the group, the last of these L—— interviews closed.[1]

[1] In describing Frederick's pyrotechnical "upside-down stunts" and the later "trimmings," the great facility with which they were executed should have been more strongly emphasized. They were all written with extraordinary rapidity and firmness.

X

THE experience at L——, while stimulating, was also fatiguing, and for several days thereafter I was tired and dull, receiving with difficulty the few communications that were attempted.

Tuesday evening, April 23d, two of Anne Lowe's friends wished to talk to her, but were told that she was busy and could not come. Mary K. answered some of their questions, concluding: "Anne sends love to you both, and says please come again soon. She is sorry she can't come now."

After giving me the twelfth Lesson, Mary K. had said: "That is the last formal lesson. The rest will be given in other ways."

"You mean through interviews and personal messages?"

"Not entirely. You will be given signed letters, by great forces."

Afterward, she mentioned these prospective communications sometimes as "letters," sometimes as "talks," but Mary Kendal told us,

May 13th, that this intention had been temporarily abandoned, as sufficient material for the book had already been given. Evidently this decision had been reached only recently, however, for an attempt to give me the first letter was frustrated on the 25th of April, and a second period of confusion and partial control by invading forces ensued.

During the morning, Mary K. prepared me for this letter, in a communication written quickly and easily, as follows:

"Men will ask the theory of the letters that are coming to them through you. This must be explained.

"As the Lessons nave been given to me to aeliver to the world through you, so the letters that are to come will be given to me by the forces from whom they come. The reason that they come through me is that I reach you more freely, when you are alone, than any other force known to you and therefore commanding your confidence. . . .

"The Lessons came from great forces combined. They represent unity of all purposes, and were framed by the co-operation and agreement of the greatest forces of each constructive purpose, to reach the consciousness of men in general terms of your plane.

"The reason that these forces do not come

to you personally is that not all of them can reach you as freely as I do. Your simile of wireless telegraphy is a good one. It does not fully explain the connection between you and me, but is as good an explanation as the progress of physical science enables you on that plane to follow. The full explanation will inevitably be possible, as physical scientists are already beginning to work toward it.

"You and I may be regarded as the receiving and sending instruments through which forces here transmit their messages. You receive from many other instruments, I send through others. But for impersonal messages you and I are most completely in accord, and thus it is that these greater forces use us as a means of communication. The first letter is ready now."

It chanced, unfortunately, that I was called away, and when I was prepared to take the letter, later in the day, almost two hours were consumed in an attempt to write the name of its author, who was described as "a leading educator." Eventually I was assured that "Matthew Alden" was correct, but, while the name was repeatedly written, I had a strong impression that it was not what Mary K. had intended to write. Reminding myself of previous difficulties in obtaining names, I tried to

believe that the delay and fatigue incident to
this effort had contributed to my doubt of its
authenticity. But the doubt remained.

The long letter which followed was also received with great difficulty and many delays,
and proved, when completed, to be a verbose
jumble of platitudes concerning educational
methods, with here and there a striking phrase.
It was signed, "Matthew Al. . . ." By this
time, I was excessively tired and could obtain
but one statement from Mary K. "You have
not the name right."

Later in the evening, I took up a pencil,
and it wrote: "Mar . . . Matthew Ald. . . ."
The name was not finished.

"Isn't Mary K. here?"

"No. No, she will return."

"She said she would be with me through
this work."

"She will again. Mary K. . . ." Illegible
lines followed.

"Is this Mary K. now?"

' No. Mary K. has gone. This is Mar. . . ."
Again the reply trailed off indeterminately.

"Mary Kendal?"

"No. Mary K. has gone. Matthew."

Eventually, failing to elicit any response
from Mary K., I asked whether Matthew had
anything to say to me, and he replied with

vague phrases, so reminiscent of the "letter" that I impatiently gave up the attempt for the day.

The next day, Friday, Matthew's signature was the only one obtainable, but I have no record of any messages. I think I refused to take them from him. Saturday morning, I tried again.

"Matthew ald. . . ."

"I want Mary K. Why isn't she here?"

"Mary K. will be ~~ret~~ . . . eternally with you."

"Then isn't she here now?"

"No, she was called away. She will come back soon."

"Was that letter from the 'educator' yours?"

"No, I am not a force for light. I am for truth and healing."

"Did you deliver it to me?"

"No."

"Then why was your name given before it?"

"Mary K. ~~to~~ . . . ~~taken~~ . . . ~~told~~ . . . ~~took~~ . . . tried to tell you I was here and would guard you. She will return soon."

"Do you know about the letter? Did she give it to me?"

"Not all of it. She will explain. I am just Mary K.'s ~~tatl~~ . . . ~~to~~ . . . ~~tr~~ . . . ~~tried~~ . . . trained substitute."

Asked how he could be her substitute, when

admittedly not of her purpose, he said: "Healing is her purpose and mine, and truth the best guard."

At this time, the Farrow mystery was still unsolved. Not until after this second prolonged experience was I given any explanation of these attacks by opposing forces, or of the conditions governing such struggles, and while I was less disquieted than upon the first occasion, I was still puzzled and uneasy, strongly suspecting interference of some kind.

That afternoon, Mrs. Gaylord and one of her daughters, passing through the city, came in for a brief talk with Frederick, and while there was at first some interference, he was soon writing with his customary clarity and vigor.

When his sister asked about a personality aggressively demanding utterance through her pencil, he said: "Not much! Don't give in to him. . . . Don't you let anybody you don't know tell you anything. It may be true and it may not, and it's not a game to play any more blindfolded than you have to be. You have to take a good deal on faith, at best. Identify anybody who comes, as far as possible."

"Can you tell me from whom that 'letter' came?" I asked.

"That letter got deteriorated in transmission. It short-circuited, so to speak, and was somewhat damaged. The next, we hope, will be better."

After my friends' departure, I caught Mary K. briefly, when she told me the source of the letter she had tried to deliver, adding that it had been too much interrupted. "Other forces tried to intervene and dominated you temporarily," she said, after which the pencil wrote only "Ma . . . Ma . . . Ma . . ." sometimes surrounding the letters with two reversed circles. I suggested Maynard, but the answer was, "No . . . Ma . . . Ma . . . Matt . . ."

"I am not a disintegrating force," was the reply to my accusation. "I am Mary K. . . ."

"Mary K. back?"

". . . no . . . her substitute. Mary K. will return soon."

"Are you sure of that?"

"Yes. Mary K. is here." This was followed by Mary K.'s characteristic and vigorous signature. "You should know me."

"It seems easy for the others to masquerade," I mentioned.

"Not to your touch," she returned, indicating a means of identification that I had hesitated to trust.

"Why do you leave me?" I demanded.

18   261

"You know I have followed light, healing, and justice all my life," was her retort. "Why doubt me now? I leave you that . . . Ma . . . Ma . . . Ma . . ."

By a curious coincidence, the names of several persons connected with these communications begin with those two letters—Mary K., Mary Kendal, Mansfield, Maynard, Margaret—and I suggested each of them in turn, before it occurred to me that "M. A." signified Matthew Alden, the usurper.

That evening was spent with Anne Lowe and her friends—Anne in one of her whimsical moods, jesting most of the time, with occasional more serious moments.

Speaking of a dog for whose death they had grieved, she said: "He came, and grew into a better force, and some day he'll make an adorable baby. Part of him, anyway. He was almost human. Every force goes on to a higher one—unless it slides back. In the end it's got to go on, so why fret and fume about a step either way? Whichever way it is, it's one step nearer the end, and the end is inevitable and fine. If people must have coasting, let them coast. They'll begin climbing that much sooner."

"Matt . . ." was written once, but with one voice we refused to talk to him. Mary K. followed, with a reference to a promise she had made to Ruth, several weeks before. Then Anne again, with an apparently clear connection.

Sunday, I was unable to get anything from Mary K. I was told she was away, doing my work. Monday morning, M. A. told me that Mary K. would be "through with the task soon," and wrote various phrases intended to be misleading. In my note-book, at this point, I find the following entry: "I am beginning to get M. A.'s messages a little more freely, but they are still slow and difficult."

Upon the departure of a visitor, late in the afternoon, I was conscious of a strong summons, and of a strange sense of turmoil and commotion. When I took up the pencil, the applied force was very strong at moments, then ceased utterly—sometimes sharply, in the middle of a word, or with a letter only half formed. Occasionally, the pencil was dragged down until it almost lay flat on the paper, and cancelations were frequent.

"Matthew Alden is destructive . . . Ma . . . M.A. . . . Matthew is destr. . . . des . . . de . . . disturbed about Mary K. She means to be the force de . . . to have . . . han . . . handle you, but she destr . . . has not done . . . been here . . . held to her purpose, and has departed to the other side of the world. She must be held firmly to her purpose."

Knowing Mary K.'s steadfastness in all things, I said that this was absurd.

"She will be ~~pursued~~ . . . ~~bett~~ . . . forced to strong pleading to be allowed to do the rest of the letters. She should be having a following of our forces. She has been detained for a long time. Matthew Alden . . . is having a battle. . . . Matthew has been defeated and . . . M.A. . . . Matthew is de . . . det . . ."

Bewildered and irritated, I demanded: "What does this mean?"

"Means that the ~~powers~~ . . . forces of de . . . construction are defeated. We have been beaten."

"I don't believe that for a minute," I said. "Or do you mean the military forces? Is Germany winning a battle to-day?"

"No, that is the least of it."

"Are you trying to tell me that Germany will win?"

"Yes, we are defeated. Her forces have reassembled, and have helped her slaughter ours." Again I said I did not believe it. "M.A. . . . Matthew is doing his best."

"You said he was defeated."

"He lost a fight."

"If you are Mary K.'s substitute, why doesn't she come to the rescue?" I asked.

"She didn't. She believes Matthew held

out. . . . Message from Mary K. Margaret,
I do. . . . I do fight for you." I asked if Mary
K. were writing. "No. Go to high forces
for help. Only be forceful for us first. Mary
K. will do her best for forces of light and
progress. Matthew is better and danger is
passing. M.A." I demanded Mary K. "Not
this time. All the forces have gathered. . . .
She should . . . said be forceful."

Saying that the whole thing seemed absurd,
I asked whether it had to do with Germany
and the war, or with the book and me—provided it had to do with anything, which I began to question.

"It is the flander . . . it is the battle . . .
book, not the godse . . . god sent war."

Amazed, I questioned: "Is God-sent war
right?"

After some delay—when one of the numerous
blanks occurred, all force being withdrawn from
the pencil—the impression of tumult instantly
ceased, leaving a sense of sudden quiet and
peace. Then—"Mary K. Mary K. Mary K."

"That feels like Mary K.," I said.

"It means Mary K., too."

"What did all that mean?"

"Meant that the forces of disintegration
have had control of you for days, at moments.
Matthew was a force for fear."

When I asked whether she had been away she wrote quickly: "No, not for one instant. He held me back, and called to your fear in accents of truth. . . . We have the forces all about us, and sometimes we are overpowered and compelled to let them through temporarily, but they can always be fought away in time."

Brisk circles of affirmation followed my suggestion that possibly this explained the Farrow episode, and she made the statement previously quoted: "We had a terrific struggle for you then. We told you the truth, but the other forces controlled the pencil."

Weeks afterward, I asked her to explain more fully this dual control, and her reply seems to me singularly illuminating.

"The connection with the pencil has no influence on your consciousness. We may control the consciousness, through purpose and its unity, even though other forces control the material instrument."

This seems not only to show why these messages are written sometimes with and sometimes without the messenger's previous knowledge of their content, but also to offer a possible explanation of phenomena of a much wider range.

To my great surprise, Mary Kendal announced herself a day or two after this, having preceded Mansfield, she said, because I was "fairly beleaguered by the enemy" in an attempt to prevent the publication of the message.

In spite of this reinforcement, however, M. A. persisted in attempts to engage my attention. On one occasion, he invited me to "try a little change" and talk to him. On another, he asked me to let him write, as he had "a long story to tell" about my husband, who was out of town. Again, he assured me that I had disappointed "them," that "they" felt that I had failed as a messenger, and that Mary K. had departed permanently. Still again, when confusion seemed to have overtaken the book project, he declared, quite frankly: "We have stopped you now. M.A."

No longer troubled by these intrusions, however, I never permitted him to use the pencil after his identity had been discovered. Occasionally I was deceived for a moment, and not infrequently it was his failure to complete a sentence or a word that betrayed him.

"He defeats himself by his fear, like all cowards," Mary K. said, one day, and when I mentioned that his messages lacked continuity, she returned: "No coward is consecutive. How could he be?"

These were by no means the last of the encounters with Matthew. Mr. Kendal arrived on the 7th of May, and a night or two later, when several of those interested in these communications were together, M. A. made his appearance again. For some time his initials followed every attempt to establish communication with our invisible friends, but eventually we obtained Mary Kendal's clear signature, and a message, slowly written, with frequent pauses, during which the personality striving to oppose her was gradually overcome. M. A.'s erratic touch was occasionally evident, lessening in strength as Mary's steady, gentle control increased.

"Come on," she said, finally. "We are ready for a little fun now, and we will leave the more serious matters until we have more truly a clear field."

Accordingly, we abandoned our intended inquiry, for the moment, resorting to persiflage, in which she took an active part, writing with increased fluency.

"Laughter is a constructive force, children," she told us, when things were going smoothly again. "Remember that when you fight fiends. . . . If we keep our touch close, and laugh like that, with real mirth, they can't get in."

Later that evening, Anne Lowe came for a moment, just to tell us, she said, that we had made a step in learning what laughter that is from the heart will do. "It is protective, constructive, curative, and the devil for devils. They can't get over, or around, or through it. That's your best weapon and your best protection, aside from fundamental purposes. Use it, and more power to your—what is it you laugh with? Diaphragm, or what?"

The next night, when conditions were normal from the first, we asked Mary Kendal about this incident, and she said: "It was just a massed attack, which will occur from time to time. They will fight as long as they exist, but the virulence and violence of their present efforts is due to our united attack on them."

An interesting and illuminating variation of these occasional sorties occurred during an interview between a man of whose personal relations and interests I have only the most casual knowledge, and a personality on the next plane whom I knew not at all.

The first messages to him, as to most of the others, concerned purpose and its unity. Apparently not convinced of the authenticity of their source, he repeatedly asked for an intimate, characteristic, personal message. Not receiving it, he asked a question relating to an entirely imaginary situation—"just to see," as he afterward explained.

The question was answered in detail, immediately followed by the statement, "Phil fears too much."

Suspecting interference, from the peculiar movement of the pencil, I asked him who Phil was, and when he replied that he knew no such person, I demanded to know who was writing.

"M.A." This signature was not complete, but the reply to a question in this connection, purporting to come from Mary K., was followed by a vigorous repetition of M. A.'s initials, inclosed in two reversed circles—his characteristic signature when in full control of the pencil.

My visitor then admitted that he had asked a fictitious question, but attempts to learn who had answered it resulted in contradictory assertions from various sources, and knowing the difficulty of re-establishing a connection once effectually broken, I refused to continue the interview.

"The integrity of the seeker," Mary K. said, the next day, "is the messenger's only protection from disintegrating force during an interview. These forces should be persistently repelled, not invited. Ignorance of their presence and power frequently opens a way for them, as in this instance. Absolute sincerity

and candor are essential to the maintenance
of a connection with constructive forces, in
these interviews."

"Forces of disintegration do not wait to be
invited," she asserted, on another occasion.
"They constantly attack, and seize the first
opportunity to take possession. We, also,
watch and call, and enter where we can. But
the idea of original sin is so strongly implanted
in the minds of most men, that an assumption
that disintegrating force can only enter where
it is invited is inevitable. It must be clearly
understood that attack by forces of disintegration does not imply weakness, or fear, or
sinful desire. It implies only a desire on the
part of the attacking force to destroy. That
there are individuals given to disintegration is
another matter. Those most desirous of construction and progress are more often attacked
by persistent, massed forces of destructive
purpose. To be conscious of this is to be pro-
tected, to some degree. For that reason, we
urge the publication of these truths, that the
struggle may no longer be waged in ignorance
and doubt and confusion."

"Does 'massed forces of destructive purpose' imply some combination, or co-operation,
or co-ordination, among disintegrating forces?"
Mary K. was asked, at another time.

"Yes, they combine every appealing force, as we do. One man may answer to doubt, fear, cupidity, and envy. Another to malice, doubt, and lust. Any forces that can reach him mass themselves in attack and call on their purposes in him to respond."

"Then there must be a considerable degree of intelligence among them. You said they would become constructive when intelligent."

"When intelligent enough. I never meant to imply that the purposes and forces of destruction are unintelligent. They are not fully intelligent. They are not balanced, not fully animated. All forces of construction comprehend destruction. No forces of destruction comprehend construction. They are intelligent and wily in destruction, but fail to apprehend its futility."

"Are they what we on this plane call uneducated, unlearned, ignorant in that sense?"

"They are sometimes found on your plane among the highly educated, learned, and powerful. Here we regard them as undeveloped forces, to be fought unceasingly until they consent to become constructive."

"You don't call that coercing your brother, do you?" I asked.

"No, we do not compel them to construct, if they would destroy by preference. We oppose them until they perceive that they must fail, and seek light. Then we accept them, instruct them, and are stronger. . . . The forces opposing us have no faith, hence no knowledge of a future. They dread destruction, fear the end of existence, deny a future, and constantly seek to destroy the inevitable."

In this connection, Mr. Kendal once asked Mary: "What do the evil forces think they're trying to do? Have they lost the great primary idea? Was there a great primary idea? Or are they just bandar-logging it around in a chaotic forest of spiritual upas-trees, screaming at anything they happen to see?"

"There was no great primary idea of destruction," she returned. "A lot of idle force gathered together, and finding itself behind the procession in strength, radiance, and beauty, began envying and coveting and backbiting, and from that to destruction is a logical and inevitable progression. Why is anybody among you envious, or malicious, or cowardly, or destructive? There is no great idea behind it. They see they are behind somebody else in something, and instead of developing what constructive power they have of their own, they hate the person who has more and try to destroy him, or his reputation, or his property. There you have concrete examples of all the idea there is in destructive purpose. It's spiritual unintelligence."

"Why did they quit Germany?" he asked, then. "Isn't the apotheosis of such personal and deterrent and soul-driving and dominating purposes just their caliber?"

"They see the forces of progress gathering among you, and know that they cannot win through Germany. She still follows their methods, but without their help, while every vibration of progressive and co-operative purpose among you enables us to help you more. So they have left her to the fruits of their union, the consequence inevitable, and hatch fresh mischief themselves."

XI

On the evening of his arrival, May 7th, Mr. Kendal asked his wife whether she could stay with us during his visit to New York, and she replied that she would outstay him, unless the forces attacking me were defeated before his departure.

"It really helps, then, for us to get together here," he inferred.

"Yes, indeed, it helps. All combination of force adds by the sum of its participation to the original amount of force combined."

Taken in conjunction with other, similar assertions in this connection—"Its force is freed and multiplied by the sum of your participation"; "For every vibration of pure constructive purpose among the Allied forces, we have added two"; "Force united is more powerful by half than similar forces separately striving"; etc.—it seems probable that these expressions were intended as figures of speech, emphasizing the increased potency of united purpose on our plane and the ability of the free forces to reinforce it in proportion to its actual vitality, rather than as mathematical statements of the exact degree to which this reinforcement and co-operation may be carried.

Mentioning that sometimes they seemed to make a distinction between purpose and force, and again to use the terms interchangeably, Mr. Kendal said he would like to know the character of each. "Is purpose like the direction of an electric current, and force like amperage and voltage?" he asked. "Or is purpose the road, and force the velocity in following it? Is purpose qualitative, and force quantitative? Is the distinction between them along some of these lines?"

"It is along all those lines," was the reply. "Purpose is the force that draws. Force is the purpose that pushes."

Like various others to whom these messages first came through me, Mr. Kendal had been trying, with some success, to obtain direct communication. Mary facetiously described his pencil as "a good burro," and mine as "a real hawse." I had thought this dialecticism differently spelled, but he reminded me that "hoss" belonged to New England, and "hawse" to Mary's native state, Kentucky.

While the pencil-point rested idly on the paper, we talked about the sensations accompanying its movement, and about the probable direction of the force propelling it. To him, the impulse seemed to come first and chiefly through the consciousness; to me, it seemed a physical force externally applied to the pencil, notwithstanding occasional consciousness of what the message would be; but we were agreed that it was difficult, at first, to be sure that the impulse was not in some unrecognized way our own.

"It has been amusing to us to see you two struggle against our psychical intrusions," Mary remarked, at this point. "We do push the pencil. We also reach the mind. Sometimes the one, sometimes the other, is what does the trick. It is easier for us to impress the mind, but harder for you to recognize that suggestion as ours. You think it's your own, and fight. Margaret is even more resistant than Manzie—perhaps because she has more responsibility to other people."

"Are present conditions—the gathering of the clans for the coming struggle—going to enable many people to do this, who have never done it before and otherwise would have been unable to do it?" he asked.

"Yes; but the danger of that is that the other forces will find their own channels, and steal and defile some of ours. So we can't

19   277

advise people to experiment, unless they can absolutely identify the force here, and only a few, comparatively, can do that."

He said that he had hesitated to ask questions of his own pencil, being unwilling to go too far in this until he had checked it up through me.

"He's scairt," she teased, before he had fairly started to speak. "You don't trust yourself or me."

Laughing, he retorted: "That's another!"

"You are right to be careful," she went on, serious again. "It's a dangerous adventure, unless you keep your balance, follow your own purpose, keep close tab on the force handling the pencil, and lean on it only spiritually. The minute advice in material things is sought, that minute there is danger."

"There's no danger that anybody can impersonate you and fool me," he declared.

"Never! The danger is that somebody might lie to you about me; or if you cease to stand on your own feet and make your own choice in matters of your plane, only then somebody might impersonate me for a moment. Sometimes I can tell you those things, but the habit of depending on them is bad for you."

A night or two later, beginning with a reply to a question concerning another subject, she returned to the discussion of the force used in conveying these communications—"a force compared to which electricity is like spring water," she said—declaring, like Frederick, that its explanation is still impossible in terms of our plane.

"There is a vital and potent force, not yet isolated—and hardly discovered—by your most advanced scientists," she told us. "It has characteristics and attractions not explainable until its discovery and analysis give rise to a new set of words. There is no adequate comparison that may be used to indicate its force, or the conditions and degrees of its variations. It has some resemblance to electricity, yet the comparison in certain cases would be misleading."

"I am talking about the force we use in moving this pencil, and to some extent in affecting your thought," she continued, when Mr. Kendal had mentioned certain recent scientific experiments of which he had read. "The scientists have long associated the power of thought with the brain, and have seriously argued that, as we could not be seen, measured, weighed, or condensed, we did not exist. We do. And we have a force at our command that cannot be explained, as yet. It can only occasionally be demonstrated as clearly as this. Electricity is the most likely to impress the man in the street as a comparison, but to argue from that as a premise would lead to misconception. At present, it must be accepted as a recognized but not understood force, only dimly perceived, as for years electricity was."

"Does it help, if we emphasize what we know of static electricity, as well as thinking of the comparison in terms of electric current? A static force in your plane, perhaps?"

"Yes, that helps; but the static force is in your plane, quite as much as here. We have more knowledge of the current, to continue the simile, but encounter static conditions both here and there, as well as counter currents here."

This would seem to offer reasons—in addition to David Bruce's explanation of the difficulties of translation when the messenger's reaction to certain word-symbols fails—for occasional delays in the transmission of these communications.

"Margaret hasn't tried us yet with an antagonistic force on your plane," she said, on another occasion. "We don't do it this way when the forces there are not harmonious."

"Is your forward sight much greater than ours?" her husband asked. "Or is it, in relation to other planes, about what ours is in regard to yours?"

"We can see the end as you have not even dreamed it yet, but our detailed knowledge is limited to two or three planes beyond ours. Even here, development is uneven, and some of us see farther than others. We are far from omniscient or omnipotent. We have advanced beyond you, our individual purposes are clear where yours are confused, we know where we are bound and why, we see much farther ahead than you can, and we work in three planes— yours as teachers, ours as laborers, and the next as students."

Referring to the statements about Russia, of which we had told him, he asked whether there were the same relative differences of opinion and judgment among them as among us, as to psychological policies to be pursued for the Great Purpose, and as to the applications of those policies on this plane.

"There are some differences of perception. Light, for example, sees shadow and desires to dispel it. Truth sees error and wishes to correct it. But, broadly speaking, the opinions are the same. The impediments in the path of progress are many. Each purpose deals with its own; Light with darkness, Truth with error, and so on. Each may work in the same field, even in the same individual, but here we work for the same ultimate purpose. We do not disagree. Each follows his own work, and recognizes the other's field."

"We have a united policy," she said, at another time, "but each our individual application of it in personal relations and messages like these. It is all intended to enlighten and inspire you, but only in certain fundamental and specific matters are we instructed what to say."

"Can you determine time there, by other than the memory of it here and by close inspection?" was another question.

"We have no time here, in your sense. We watch you, and remember, but we lose track of you, sometimes."

Mr. Kendal then said—explaining his phrase, "close inspection"—that he thought they saw time dimly, as we see through water or through fog.

"Is memory with you as acute as answers to some of these questions seem to indicate?" one of us inquired.

"Not of material things, generally. We don't pay much attention to them, unless they interfere with purpose. Just now they are interfering a good deal—or were, before the war, which is itself a material manifestation of purpose." We said that we should have thought this interference in full force still, and she continued: "The real interference, from our point of view, came before the war, when the world outside of Germany was too much occupied in pursuit of material things to see what was happening. They failed even to see Germany's intention. Much less did they discover their own danger, of which Germany's purpose, materially, was the least. The war woke them up by degrees, fortunately, or there would be no use telling them this."

A question concerning the possibility of communicating with a person recently departed from this plane, was met with the statement that he had "free communion" still to learn. This expression had been used several times by others, and now I asked: "Mary, what is free communion?"

"You don't think we vocalize our talk, do you?"

Mansfield suggested that when a man found himself suddenly without his material veil, he must be at a loss how to proceed, and asked whether that was what she meant.

"Not entirely. The veil isn't missed particularly, but there is a . . . a. . . ."

"Difference of medium?" he asked. "Like a water-color artist who can't paint in oil?"

"That's it."

"Referring to your assertion in March that truth is absolute," he said, "is not truth itself relative on this plane? Truth as a statement of eternal law is absolute, but when applied to concrete facts and ideas, it changes from time to time? That is, a concrete statement which expressed the relations of certain mundane conditions to the eternal verities in B.C. 1000, would not necessarily be a correct statement of the relations of corresponding conditions to those verities in the year 1900 A.D."

"That is the idea on which this whole revelation is based," she returned. "These things have always been true. They would not have sounded true in the year one, any more than a lot of the 'truths' of that day are true now."

A night or two after this, he said he would like more light on the practical application of these principles, especially those in relation to freedom. "How, for instance, would you go about helping a school?" he asked. "Take, as concrete examples, a University like ——, its Faculty held in subjection by hidebound trustees, and the proposed People's University, to be governed from day to day by plebiscite or referendum, with no defined policy or procedure beyond a general idea of freedom. 'You may lead a horse to water, but you can't

make him drink.' Should the construction of
the trough be left to chance, or should it be
planned carefully? In other words, should
mundane provision and prevision be employed
in building it?"

"It has been said already that men must
first learn to think, and to govern themselves,
before they can be free." It was Mary K.
who answered. "If experience were not taken
into consideration, progress would be impossible. Mundane prevision and provision is
essential to all constructive activity on your
plane. Opinions will differ as to ways and
means of applying principles of progress.
The first way to help a school. is to establish unity among the teachers. Not only
unity of purpose, but a certain large unity of
method, that one may not tear down what
his brother builds. Ideals of freedom have
been confused by men resenting the first law
of freedom—discipline. Lack of discipline,
carried to its logical conclusion, would return
the world to chaos. The school that is free
in its teaching must be carried on by disciplined
teachers, united in a purpose of progress clearly
recognized and agreed upon, to teach discipline
that the minds of men may dare to be free."

"The idea underlying that, I take it, is that
as the athlete whose body is thoroughly trained

and co-ordinated dares to jump an abyss, without fear of falling, so the man whose mind and spirit are disciplined can jump an intellectual abyss, without losing balance or sanity."

"Yes. And as a man trained to carry great weights on his shoulders must be trained to it from youth, so the man who would carry government and freedom of thought must train his mind to carry its weight—not alone to hold it briefly, but to carry it on."

"Is it true, then," he asked, "that safe freedom and constructive freedom are only possible after prior discipline and self-control?"

"How can undisciplined freedom be safe or constructive? It makes the wilderness. It makes the jungle. It makes the uncharted and devouring sea."

XII

ONE day, about the middle of May, discussing these manifestations over a luncheon table, a man who described himself as "a sympathetic agnostic" mentioned that while all those on the next plane reported that they were busy, none to his knowledge had told just what they were doing.

At that time, we had received several statements concerning their activities. Frederick had spoken of his efforts in connection with "a pro - German newspaper editor." Maynard Holt's mother had told us that she worked "with undeveloped purposes, here before their time." It had been said of a famous editor: "He is for Justice. . . . He is one of the forces determining the grouping of the newly arrived." Anne Lowe had said: "I handle children. Some of them thought they were grown up when they left you." And the work of the healers, in receiving and soothing "war-stricken forces," had been repeatedly mentioned.

However, with the comment of the "sympathetic agnostic" in mind, we asked Mary Kendal, apropos of some allusion to the healers on her plane, whether she could tell us of their work in detail.

"You have already seen that our ability to be specific, even about things here, is dependent on your ability to understand conditions of our plane," she reminded us. "As fast as we can, we give it to you. But as well explain the operation of wireless telegraphy to an illiterate 'cracker,' as to try to explain healing, as we understand and practise it, to the person unprepared by thought and study of these truths."

The next day, in another city, Frederick, writing through a member of his family, said that he had been doing some work in developing some spirits who had "let their lowest tendencies be their guiding force."

"They were men who were very unhappy, because they had left the world before they were ready, and did not know what this life meant," he said.

"Had they recently gone over?" he was asked.

"Yes, not very long on this side. They were so bewildered that they thought they were in some kind of dream that they could not wake from. They had been sick, but not long enough to let them get any idea of death, or light after death, so they were sorry to come over."

"Do they call you teacher?"

"No, just a friend."

Replying to a question about a specific activity on this plane, he said: "I can tell you that a lot of those things that seem bewildering are not important enough to be doing what we call work here."

"What do you call work?"

"Conscious development of spiritual forces."

A month later, a question about a woman known here as a sculptor brought the following reply from David Bruce.

"She is working with a development of the purpose of production, which is the foundation that underlay her work there. She is producing force by developing the undeveloped producers."

Probably the most specific information yet received by any of our small group concerning the practical application of these principles to the affairs of our plane, came through Maynard Holt.

"My work lies principally with business men on your plane," he said, one day, to a family connection. "We are much concerned about the lack of co-operation among persons of constructive tendencies, and my own job is to apply this force we cannot fully explain to you, in any way that will influence men or women toward co-operation. Sometimes we use it to suggest a new idea. Sometimes we use it to so direct apparently consequential circumstances and events that the person we wish to influence gets an object lesson."

In support of this is a statement of his made in April. While writing a long message, most of which was intimately personal, he indicated his interest in business conditions, and urged a greater and more far-seeing co-operation among business men. In the midst of a sentence the pencil stopped, creating a long delay. Failing, after repeated efforts, to transmit the word he had attempted, he drew a series of singularly uniform arches across the whole width of the paper.

After puzzling over it a moment, I drew a line above the arches, and said, perceiving no significance in the symbol: "That looks like a viaduct."

"That's what I mean," he resumed, vigorously, and proceeded with an elaboration of his theme, comparing co-operation to a viaduct.

"In the end, the forces for progress will cross to all lands by that viaduct," he continued, "and those who balk and refuse it will be diverted and delayed by following old paths through the tortuous chasm of competitive destruction. Not that we discourage competition. The individual organization, like the individual man, must follow its purpose and develop its force, but . . . competition at its best is entirely friendly and constructive. Boys have it taught them in the simplest form in college sports. There it is personal, but co-operative in the development of college spirit. Each man does his best for himself and his own record, but loyally and cheerfully supports against opposing forces the more successful man who is of his own group. With increasing responsibilities, temptations and difficulties increase, but experience should bring ability to meet them. The code of school and college forces may be developed and applied to business and productive forces. This is the first application of college training to competitive business."

Afterward, when Mr. Kendal had expressed his cordial sympathy with the theory of co-operation, widely applied, Maynard said: "That's where the college team has won and the union has failed. The union was good in conception, but has made for the suppression of individual development, where the college team encourages it."

Later still, following a conversation concerning national economics and international commerce after the war, he said:

"Co-operation is moral. Commercial supremacy is material. Material success is constructive only if permanent, and permanent only if constructive. Until co-operation for permanent progress becomes a principle of international as well as national purpose, there will be little actual progress toward permanent peace, or lasting prosperity.

"As the college boy works first for his own power, but most for his team, and first, last and all the time for clean athletics, so the business man should work first for his unit, definitely for his country's welfare, but first, last and always for clean co-operation with all who make for the world's progress.

"The exponents of national supremacy at the expense of world progress are exactly in the position of the exponents of personal prosperity at the expense of national welfare. The situations are analogous to a degree as yet comprehended by few men.

"It took many years to convince the manufacturer that increased production would follow shorter hours and improved working conditions. It took many years to convince merchants that decreased cost and increased profit followed combination of forces. It took some time to convince financiers and manufacturers that success, not failure, would follow the co-operation of competing concerns in the foreign field. Yet it is now recognized that all these things are true and practicable. No less —even more—is it practicable to unite world forces of progress in commerce as they are united now in war, the fight at all times being for construction and development, against destruction and regression.

"This cannot be done in a day or a year, but this is the goal toward which enlightened forces should move. It may sound Utopian now. So did model factories and tenements, a few years ago. Their advocates were scoffed at and discredited. Now, the manufacturer who fails to provide healthful working conditions for his operatives is called short-sighted and pig-headed, and cheats himself twice, while cheating his employees once.

"Co-operation is the basic principle of all progress, and the point at which it stops is the measure of strength of man or nation. The nation that refuses to co-operate for progress is a nation confessing itself deterrent."

Again, in June, Maynard returned to this subject, saying that men must become "strong enough to let the other fellow live and prosper, without fearing him." After mentioning "fear of what may come, or lust for what may be seized," as motives making for destruction, he added: "Neither is constructive or progressive, and neither can win in the end."

"We have purpose to progress beyond the vision of man," he went on, "but even material progress, to be constructive and permanent, must be governed by a vision beyond the day. We are trying to extend that vision.

"Co-operation in individual enterprise has succeeded. Co-operation in national enterprise would succeed no less. More and more, men are recognizing the value of united effort in commercial enterprise, however long it took the truth to dawn. Must other centuries pass, other wars be fought, other dynasties rise and fall, before the larger truth ushers in a new day? Will co-operation in business, co-operation in war, teach them to study and practise co-operation in world welfare and progress? Will they learn that it is not only in war that a weakened Belgium means an endangered England, that a hungry France means short rations in America, that a link weakened means the chain weak?

"How many times must this premise be demonstrated before the argument is carried to its logical conclusion, and national co-operation, free and voluntary, provide for the good of one by protecting and developing all?

"This is not a Utopian fantasy. It is common sense."

XIII

Talking about the Lessons one day, Mr. Kendal mentioned his impression that Zoroaster had said something approaching the first one in theory, and then asked, a whimsical gleam in his eye: "Mary, has Professor James said anything about Zoroaster in this connection?"

"Manzie, Mr. James has no philosophical library here to refer to," was the prompt retort. She told us, however, that he would soon come himself to talk to this former pupil of his, adding a characteristic glint of humor in the assurance that he would then give "a demonstration of a philosopher simplified to a force."

A night or two afterward (May 13th), she announced: "Manzie, here is Mr. James."

There was a brief delay, and when the pencil moved again, it was with a changed application of force and a new movement, the first words being personal. Referring to an early period in his own investigation of psychic phenomena, he said:

"Youth, in its nearness to inspiration, sometimes sees more clearly than age, with its
academic dependence upon theory and precedent and what men call the wisdom of experience. When this wisdom is based on
perception, conscious or otherwise, of eternal
purpose, it transcends the vision of youth.
But when it is based on perception of physical
phenomena and the accumulated theories of
other men, youth has an inspiration and a
faith that leads it, all unknowing, to the brink
of great mysteries." This was followed by an
allusion to those "befogged in precedent, physical phenomena, and intellectual theory," who
were "unable to follow where they should have
led."

"There has seemed to be a good deal of
genuine feeling underlying the humorous persiflage through the pencil about the scientific
state of mind," Mr. Kendal suggested. "Hasn't
the time come when we can reach the scientific
type of mind? And isn't it worth while to do
so? And if so, what is the best psychological
line of attack?"

"The scientist is not by any means hopeless,
but like many men in your plane, he is over-
balanced and therefore unbalanced by physical
considerations. Physical phenomena are of
vital importance in your life, and their study

and analysis has led to a degree of material progress which would have been incredible to the third—and all but incredible to the second —generation back. It is only because scientists have persisted in the study of physical phenomena that you are enabled to understand in some part what is now being given you. The misapprehension has been that physical phenomena alone could be recognized. Those who have believed that have denied the existence of the greatest and most persistent of all forces. Attempts to explain spiritual phenomena by physical formulæ have been found unsuccessful by every one save those who took refuge in denial of the thing that moved them to deny, the eternal and indestructible purpose.

"When to their laboratories scientists bring perception of spiritual phenomena exceeding any material manifestation known to man in strength and significance, then they may hope to discover and develop a force beside which all known forces are insignificant. Science is the ladder by which life may quickly ascend, but until science recognizes a spiritual force as the one essential force, of which all other forces are incidental phenomena, progress must be limited."

"Then, generally speaking," Mr. Kendal

said, "perhaps the most effective appeal to scientists would be the appeal to scientific ambition."

"Always the most effective means to win any man to anything is to appeal to his purpose. If it be personal, appeal to his vanity. If it be progressive, appeal to his eagerness. If it be intellectual, pique his curiosity. Scientists, like others, are divided in purpose."

"We have been much interested in the decisive definiteness with which our friends on that plane have been able to classify the purposes of persons here," Mr. Kendal mentioned. "Is this as clear to you as physical characteristics are to us, and as quickly determined?"

"Yes, and in much the same way. We see motive and intention and their variations as you see physical appearance, vitality and its variations. We see disintegrating moral factors more clearly than you see physical ills. We judge of purpose by its vitality and persistence under strain, precisely as you judge of physical health by its vitality under strain and by its persistence in spite of occasional disease."

"Then you see disintegrating force as the scientist sees germs?" Cass inquired. "As disease?"

"No, we see them as foes. I speak here

only of the way we judge purpose. There is no diseased purpose. There may be struggle between more or less intelligent forces, but in using the simile of physical health, I did it in a limited sense."

"Is there an inherent reason for the different types of philosophies?" Mr. Kendal now questioned. "That is, the Nirvana-oblivion type in the Orient, as contrasted with the hell-fire-and-brimstone type in the Occident. If inherent, is its cause geographical, intellectual, biological, or what?"

"A little of all of them. Philosophies are the outgrowth of conditions, physical, moral and geographical—and therefore to some extent biological—to a much greater degree than is generally recognized. It has been said that food makes the man. To a greater degree, environment makes the philosopher."

"May we publish this as coming from you?"

"Certainly. I am here for that purpose. . . . Light and Progress are my purposes, and teaching still my work."

After a few lines of purely personal significance, this was signed: "William James."

XIV

Of the messages that may be quoted, there remain only a few detached statements, removed from their personal context, but reproduced because of their general interest or significance.

"Don't worry about C——" was one bit of specific advice, given in March, before any of the Lessons had been received. "She will have her troubles, but she must dree her own weird. You might save her some pain, but life's purpose may not be taught. It must be fought for, with blood and sweat. Let C—— get her wounds in her own way. You may then soothe the pain. But don't try to spare her the fight. That has to do with the larger questions of life and eternity."

"'Life's purpose may not be taught,' but the laws underlying the search for it may be?"

"Of course. We are trying now to wake the world to consciousness that these laws exist. Most people, broadly speaking, have forgotten them, in the general contempt for laws where

they are not enforced, and in the general
hatred of them where they are enforced in
oppression and fear."

A few days later, another person, writing of
another and much younger girl, said: "She
may have a hard time over the conflicting
purposes. Everybody does. But with you
to give her a foundation, I do not fear for her.
. . . Her struggles will only make her stronger.
Do not try to save her from pain. Remember
that it is her mother who says this. Let her
meet life fully and work her way upward.
She will always yield in the end to the sublime
purpose."

On a later occasion, this same person said:
"We help all we can, but even when you want
us to, we are unwilling to hold back the larger
and vital development in order to hasten some
smaller conclusion. Even when the small conclusion is important to you, it must be your
own choice that helps you; and if the choice
is wrong at the moment, it still helps in the
end."

"She's too sympathetic for her own good,"
was said of another young woman. "She'd do
the vicarious atonement act for all creation,
if she could. What she needs is to have this
purpose business driven into her. Every fellow has to do his own fighting, and his own

atonement, and his own climbing, and take what's coming to him while he does it. She's always trying to soften the path and take the swipes herself, and it can't be done. She gets the blow and the strain and the struggle, all right, but it impedes her and gets the other fellow nowhere. It helps nobody to save them the consequences of their own choice. The way to help is to call to their constructive purpose and give them a chance. If they choose not to take it, then let them take all the consequence that's coming. If that doesn't teach them, there's nothing more to do, except to turn them over to somebody who can arouse their purpose, if they have any. Anyhow, making a buffer of yourself just batters up good material for no gain in force or purpose."

Again, another person to another group. "Let any fighting force do his own fighting. Suggest, enlighten, encourage, but don't try to carry the burden of another's life. You can't hurry their development, and you impede your own and that of others of your own purpose. . . . You are like the fellow in the fable, who finished by carrying not only the pack, but the donkey, too. It's a very sweet and unselfish disposition, but do you think it improves the donkey for his station in life? Not that I'm calling S—— a donkey, but like all mankind, he carries a pack. You can't carry both, and he won't learn to apply his force evenly here if you do it for him there. Lots of people develop unevenly and have to even up somewhere. Why delay the process by vicarious labor, especially when it only exhausts you and doesn't develop his muscles any? Selah!"

"You can train O—— to carry physical temptations, if you begin early," a man said, writing of his nephew. "Don't let him yield to impulse or desire when it is destructive. Make him build his body first, as a boy. Make him respect it and its promise. That's a bully thing for a boy to know at the beginning. He reasons from that to other things. A boy is a brute first, but a thinking brute. If he respects the flesh, he respects all things in time."

"What is my purpose?" a young man asked, one day.

"Building. You are going to be 'him that hath.' Build with your possessions. Begin the foundation now. Build. . . . Build as a producer, or as a healer, or in any way that makes for progress, keeps you growing, develops forces for construction, and gives the other fellows a chance to do their best also. . . . Not for yourself alone, but for all who may climb by your ladder of opportunity."

Maynard Holt, writing to a friend here, spoke of him as a good fighter, and when this person said that he would not have been able to fight at all, but for the little hand of a lady on the next plane, Maynard returned: "I know you fought hard, though in darkness, before you found that hand. That's one reason we count on you now. A man who will fight continuously in darkness is a . . . a . . ." The pencil paused, and after futile efforts to proceed, retraced its path, apparently to cross out again and again the last letter. We were talking and paid no attention to its movement, but when it ceased again, we discovered that Maynard had drawn a five-pointed star. Then he proceeded: ". . . luminary of force himself, when light breaks."

There were many interesting characterizations, both of persons on this plane and of those on the next.

"E—— is a fine force, but A—— is a force multiplied and refined to power," was said of one couple.

A striking example of the determination of our "fantom friends" to convey their meaning despite obstacles, was indicated when some one had told me, during an interview, of a boy's objection to his mother's activity in one of the recent "drives" connected with war work, on the ground that it "made her conspicuous."

"M—— is an entirely tra . . . trem . . . tr . . . normal and tra . . . tremulous youth, where his mother and sister are concerned," was his father's humorous comment.

Apparently, in this case, the connection was imperfect, no intimation of his meaning reaching me, and only by altering the form of his sentence was he able to get it written.

"Miss T—— has much to learn and much to suffer before a teaching based on unity of force or purpose will reach her forcefully," we were told, on another occasion. "She must learn the shallows of self before she can sound the depths of individuality, in the larger and eternal interpretation of the word."

Following one of the numerous discussions of Germany and her purposes, a question about a man of German parentage brought this reply: "B—— is American. The national taint of docility is not in him."

The meaning of purpose and its application was stated many times in many ways. One of the most characteristic of these expressions came from a famous humorist.

"There are things brewing here and among you there," he said, "that are going to make the wars of the tribes of Hohenzollern, Hapsburg and Mephisto look like a village prayer meeting. The carnage of Verdun and Mons and the whole show since his little nibs was assassinated is a picayune proposition compared to the losses of time, purpose, force and saving grace that we're all going to feel, if we can't wake you people up to pull together against the devil's crew."

Some one asked whether a husband and wife, not too congenial in this life, were together there, and was told that he was "flocking with birds of his own feather," and that she had "peacefully and tranquilly found her own." Another member of this family group was with neither of the others, it was said, "because she found her very own, for which they were only a substitute."

"Have you seen Jim? Is there any feeling about his wife's marrying again?" was a question which will interest many persons.

"Jim is here and very happy. He has no resentment, and wishes Alice to be happy. They are both of the forces of progress, but not of just the same purpose. They harmonize, but do not touch."

Again, some one asked whether one party to an uncongenial marriage regretted the other's rejoining him so soon.

"She didn't," was the reply. "He hasn't seen

her yet, and won't. He is willing to work with her purpose, but not eager to touch her force."

"What about Laura?" a woman asked.

"She is coming to us soon, but do not be afraid, dear. She will be tenderly met and guided, and will be much nearer you all, much happier and more helpful, than she is now. Never grieve again for death. It is birth, and so happy."

Within a few weeks, this came to pass.

When I asked Mary K. for a message for a mother bereaved by war, she said: "Tell her we will send for her when he has grown accustomed enough to talk to her. Tell her that he is cared for tenderly and guided, and that she must not grieve. She hurts him and herself. Make her understand that she can help him by knowing that he lives and loves her and is near her, and that it is part of her work as a mother to help him in this . . . to find his purpose more quickly through her love."

We were afterward told that he had not yet learned the "free communion," but that from the moment his mother began to "lift her spirit to meet his," this young man's development was hastened.

Frequently, when telling about these revelations, I have been asked: "What do they say about reincarnation?"

"There is no possible reincarnation," Mary K. said, when I referred the question to her. "That is a dream of the Orient. The idea of reincarnation is regressive. Not destructive, but deterrent. Not progressive. It is born of bodily desire."

"Is it like the desire of old men for youth?"

"More. It is a mask, covering material desire with spiritual semblance. It is taught from this plane by deterrent or partly deterrent forces, lacking free vision."

In another connection, but with similar meaning, David Bruce said: "Some persons hide their love of the flesh by an exaggerated expression of spirituality, and then think of ways of insisting on the flesh."

Similarly, writing through her husband's pencil, Mary Kendal said, when he asked her what had become of persons like Cæsar, Luther, Cobden, Archimedes, and others in general: "There is a great difference in the length of time people stay in this plane nearest to that of the earth, which depends not only on the stage of development which they have attained when they come here, but also on the character of work they are best fitted to do. If they can be of more use in direct or indirect contact with your plane, they stay here sometimes many years, as you measure time; but if they are retarded in their development when they arrive here, they have a long road to travel before they can go on to any other plane. There is no such thing as transmigration of souls as you understand it, but that idea is akin to what actually does happen, in the sense that such individualities have to pass through stages of development which are relatively inferior in status to those that they might enter into, coming from your plane, if they had made greater progress there, or had fought a better fight on that plane."

When he said that his idea in asking about specific individuals was to get concrete instances by which to check up the general law, she returned: "The danger in that is that your idea of what those individuals really were is very apt to be wrong, and starting from wrong premises you could hardly avoid reaching wrong conclusions. . . . Martin Luther was a mixture of purposes. He did great work for progress in fighting the conventions and binding tendency of ecclesiasticism in his times, but he had personal motives which were deterrent, and which he spent a long time in working out when he left that plane." Of Napoleon she said: "There have been few instances of greater prostitution of great talents and great opportunity in history, and he paid

—and is paying—the penalty, or the consequence."

To the many inquiries as to how direct communication may be established between persons here and the dear ones gone before, this message of David Bruce's to his wife contains the briefest and most comprehensive answer.

She said: "I wonder what he's going to tell me?"

"I'm going to tell you to be calm and serene of spirit, no matter what seems to be happening to disturb you. Most of the disturbing factors of individual life on your plane are ephemeral—things of the moment and of the place. Others are more important than they seem. I am not always able to tell you about them. It delays you, instead of helping you, when the decision is not your own. One way that I can truly help when you are troubled is by what we can best describe as the free communion. When you are perturbed in spirit and full of doubt, it is difficult for us to reach you. . . . Open the door of spiritual force to forces here, and we can always help. That is what we hope to establish as a recognized truth in your life there. That a force as yet unknown to science is operating between the planes, and can be developed and used in your life there—to a less degree than in ours, but still with great effect. It is for this that we work in this communion, which is more definite to you now and less so to us. We know the limits to which material manifestation like this is confined, and are eager to teach you gradually the freer and fuller way."

XV

"A THOUGHT that will occur to many persons is that the truths we endeavor to teach are not entirely new.

"Truth is fundamental and eternal. There is no new truth; there is only new understanding and application of truth that has always existed. No great teacher has ever told new truth. No great teacher has ever told truth in a new way, until the older teachings had begun to lose their hold on the minds of men. No great teacher has ever found an audience for his new interpretation of truth, until the minds of men had groped through darkness toward a light dimly perceived, if at all.

"The time is ripe now for the crystallization of new application of eternal truth. Men hunger for bread of the spirit, and thirst for the waters of eternity. This is the answer of eternal forces to their search, and it comes, for the first time, not through a teacher or a prophet, but through a human instrument sensitive to a high degree to the influence of the force that is life's motive power.

"There are many conditions affecting the application of that force in these communications, that cannot now be explained; many conditions influencing its direction, that you do not understand. Some day your scientists will discover and prove by experiment certain laws now unrecognized, and these days of doubt and scoffing will disappear in a past filled with denial and discouragement of almost every discovery now called modern and progressive.

"Two things only we have striven for through you: to prove to a group of intelligent persons that this force exists and may be practically applied between your plane and ours, and to warn mankind of the nature and eternal import of impending struggles. We have more to tell when they are ready to listen, and upon the choice of them who hear this truth the immediate progress of the world depends. It is a warning to unite and prepare for combat.

"This is the truth. Heed it.

"MARY K."

June 13, 1918.

THE END

9 781444 665314